You don't have to spend a lot to eat well. That's the concept behind this guide, and it's never been truer – or more important – than it is right now.

Since launching Zagat Survey 30 years ago, we've seen the restaurant industry continually improve its ability to deliver good value. These days, there are bargains to be found at every level of the dining spectrum, from high-end restaurants offering prix fixe deals to the exploding ranks of low-budget ethnics. And of course there are abundant classic low-cost eateries (BBQs, burger joints, coffee shops and pizzerias).

While the current economic outlook may be uncertain, one thing's for sure: It will only accelerate restaurateurs' efforts to find more ways to deliver a bigger bang for your dining buck.

The restaurants listed in this guide represent a wide range of cuisines and styles, offering options to suit all kinds of tastes and occasions. We've also included tips for getting the most from your dining dollars. So even if you're tightening your belt financially, you may have to let it out a few notches after digging into the many dining deals that await on the coming pages.

Enjoy!

Nina and Tim Zagat

New York City
Dining Deals

Published and distributed by
Zagat Survey, LLC
4 Columbus Circle
New York, NY 10019
T: 212.977.6000
E: nycdiningdeals@zagat.com
www.zagat.com

The reviews published in this guide
are based on public opinion
surveys. The numerical ratings
reflect the average scores given by
all survey participants who voted on
each establishment. The text is
based on direct quotes from, or fair
paraphrasings of, participants'
comments. Phone numbers,
addresses and other factual
information were correct to the best
of our knowledge when published
in this guide.

© 2008 Zagat Survey, LLC
ISBN-13: 978-1-60478-131-1
ISBN-10: 1-60478-131-9
Printed in the
United States of America

Contents

Ratings & Symbols

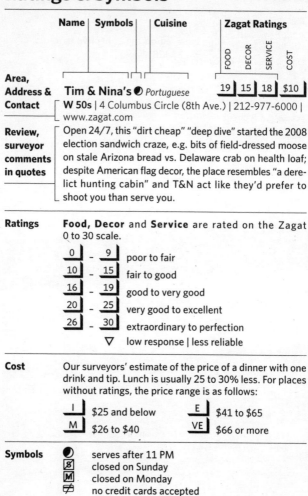

	Name	**Symbols**	**Cuisine**	**Zagat Ratings**			
				FOOD	DECOR	SERVICE	COST

Area, Address & Contact

Tim & Nina's ◕ *Portuguese* | 19 | 15 | 18 | $10 |

W 50s | 4 Columbus Circle (8th Ave.) | 212-977-6000 | www.zagat.com

Review, surveyor comments in quotes

Open 24/7, this "dirt cheap" "deep dive" started the 2008 election sandwich craze, e.g. bits of field-dressed moose on stale Arizona bread vs. Delaware crab on health loaf; despite American flag decor, the place resembles "a derelict hunting cabin" and T&N act like they'd prefer to shoot you than serve you.

Ratings

Food, Decor and **Service** are rated on the Zagat 0 to 30 scale.

0 – 9	poor to fair
10 – 15	fair to good
16 – 19	good to very good
20 – 25	very good to excellent
26 – 30	extraordinary to perfection
∇	low response	less reliable

Cost

Our surveyors' estimate of the price of a dinner with one drink and tip. Lunch is usually 25 to 30% less. For places without ratings, the price range is as follows:

| I | $25 and below | E | $41 to $65 |
| M | $26 to $40 | VE | $66 or more |

Symbols

◕	serves after 11 PM
Ⱬ	closed on Sunday
Ⰼ	closed on Monday
⊅	no credit cards accepted

About This Survey

We are pleased to present our first-ever **New York City Dining Deals,** covering 449 eateries. Like all our guides, this one is based on the collective opinions of avid consumers – 38,128 all told.

WHO PARTICIPATED: Input from these enthusiasts forms the basis for all the ratings and reviews in this guide (their comments are shown in quotation marks). Collectively they bring roughly 6.6 million annual meals' worth of experience to this guide. We sincerely thank each of them – this book is really "theirs."

ABOUT ZAGAT: This marks our 30th year reporting on the shared experiences of consumers like you. Today we have over 350,000 surveyors and now cover airlines, bars, dining, entertaining, fast food, golf, hotels, movies, music, resorts, shopping, spas, theater and tourist attractions in over 100 countries.

INTERACTIVE: Up-to-the-minute news about restaurant openings plus menus, photos and more are free on **ZAGAT.com** and the award-winning **ZAGAT.mobi** (for web-enabled mobile devices). They also enable one-click reserving at thousands of places.

AVAILABILITY: Zagat guides are available in all major bookstores as well as on **ZAGAT.com.** To access our content when on the go, visit **ZAGAT.mobi** or **ZAGAT TO GO.** With just one click, you'll be talking to 40,000 restaurants, nightspots and hotels.

VOTE AND COMMENT: There is always room for improvement, thus we invite your suggestions about any aspect of our performance. Just contact us at **nycdiningdeals@zagat.com.** To join any of our surveys visit **ZAGAT.com.** In exchange for sharing your experiences, you'll get a **free copy** of the resulting guide when published.

New York, NY
December 1, 2008

Nina and Tim

Nina and Tim Zagat

Dining Tips

In the current economic climate, bargain-hunting has taken on greater urgency. While NYC dining can be expensive, locals know great food can be found at modest tabs. This guide lists 449 places where you'll find good buys (also visit **ZAGAT.com** and **ZAGAT.mobi** for more suggestions). Here are some tips to get the best for less:

- Some of the most revered high-end restaurants in town offer bargain prix fixe menus that allow you to experience them for a fraction of their normal cost. See lists on page 10.

- Lunch is cheaper than dinner – by as much as 25 to 30%. The more expensive the restaurant, the more you're likely to save.

- Outer borough eateries are normally far less costly than those in Manhattan and continue to grow in quality and variety. See list on page 12.

- Take advantage of NYC's Restaurant Weeks (usually in January and June), when hundreds of the city's finest restaurants offer greatly reduced prices.

- Classic cheap-eat places – pizzerias, BBQs, burger joints, upscale diners, noodle shops and myriad ethnic places – are on the rise and offer some of the best values in town.

- Certain neighborhoods offer a concentration of low-cost eateries, e.g., the Bronx's Arthur Avenue, Queens' Jackson Heights, Manhattan's Chinatown, Gramercy's "Curry Hill", among others.

- Some of the city's big-name chefs have recently opened scaled-down, low-cost venues, to wit, Daniel Boulud's **Bar Boulud,** Laurent Tourondel's **BLT Burger,** Tom Valenti's **West Branch** and the new lounge at Sirio Maccioni's **Le Cirque.**

- By adopting healthier dining habits, you can trim your budget as well as your waistline. For example, fill up on lightly dressed salads and non-cream-based soups, split portions, and finally, avoid alcohol and desserts.

- As for wine, ask the sommelier for the best wine "at the lowest price." Given markups from three- to tenfold, you're throwing your money away if you select a pricey vintage.

Dining Deals by Category

BAKERY/DESSERT

Amy's Bread
Bouchon Bakery
ChikaLicious
City Bakery
Clinton St. Baking Co.
Ferrara
La Bergamote
La Flor Bakery
Le Pain Quotidien
Once Upon a Tart

BBQ

Blue Smoke
Daisy May's
Dinosaur BBQ
Fette Sau
Hill Country
Rack & Soul
RUB BBQ
Smoke Joint
Virgil's Real BBQ
Wildwood BBQ

BURGERS & HOT DOGS

brgr
burger joint
Corner Bistro
DuMont
Five Guys
Gray's Papaya
Island Burgers
Papaya King
Rare B&G
Shake Shack
67 Burger
Stand

CHICKEN ROASTERS

Coco Roco
Dirty Bird to-go
El Malecon
Flor de Mayo
Mancora
Peter's Since 1969
Pio Pio

CHINESE

Chef Ho's
Fuleen Seafood
Grand Sichuan
Joe's Shanghai
Nice Green Bo
Oriental Garden
Peking Duck
Phoenix Garden
Spicy & Tasty
Tang Pavilion

DELIS

Barney Greengrass
Carnegie Deli
Ess-a-Bagel
Friedman's Deli
Katz's Deli
Leo's Latticini
Mill Basin Deli
Pastrami Queen
2nd Ave Deli
Zabar's Cafe

DIM SUM

Café Evergreen
Dim Sum Go Go
East Manor
Golden Unicorn
Jing Fong

Mandarin Court
Our Place
Ping's Seafood
Sweet-n-Tart
X.O.

DINERS

Brooklyn Diner
Comfort Diner
Diner
Empire Diner
Junior's
Teresa's
Tom's

FAMILY STYLE

Carmine's
Dominick's
Don Peppe
Patricia's
Piccolo Angolo
Pisticci

ICONIC PLACES

Carmine's | *Italian*
Carnegie Deli | *Deli*
Corner Bistro | *Burgers*
Empire Diner | *Diner*
Gray's Papaya | *Hot Dog*
Grimaldi's | *Pizza*
John's Pizzeria | *Pizza*
Junior's | *Diner*
Katz's Deli | *Deli*
Virgil's Real BBQ | *BBQ*

INDIAN

Banjara
Bukhara Grill
Chennai Garden
Chola
Indus Valley
Kati Roll Co.

Saravanaas
Surya
Utsav
Yuva

ITALIAN

Al Di La
Arté Café
Bamonte's
Becco
Crispo
Da Andrea
Fiorentino's
Frank
La Lanterna di Vittorio
Sette Enoteca

KOREAN

Cho Dang Gol
Do Hwa
Dok Suni's
Gahm Mi Oak
Kang Suh
Kum Gang San
Mandoo Bar
Moim
Momofuku Ssäm
Persimmon

NOODLE SHOPS

Great NY Noodle
Ippudo
Kampuchea
Minca
Momofuku Noodle
New Bo-Ky
Pho Viet Huong
Rai Rai Ken
Ramen Setagaya
Soba-ya

PIZZA

- Adrienne's Pizza
- Artichoke Basille's
- Denino's
- Di Fara
- Franny's
- Grimaldi's
- La Pizza Fresca
- Lombardi's
- Lucali
- Pizza Gruppo

PUB FOOD

- Eight Mile Creek
- Elephant & Castle
- J.G. Melon
- Joe Allen
- Landmark Tavern
- O'Neals'
- P.J. Clarke's
- Public House
- Spotted Pig
- Walker's

THAI

- Erawan
- Jaiya Thai
- Joya
- Kuma Inn
- Land
- Pam Real Thai
- Pukk
- Sookk
- Sripraphai
- Wondee Siam

TOP CHEF BARGAINS

- Bar Boulud (Daniel Boulud)
- bar Q (Anita Lo)
- Benoit (Alain Ducasse)
- Blaue Gans (Kurt Gutenbrunner)
- BLT Burger (Laurent Tourondel)
- Matsugen (Jean-Georges Vongerichten)
- Otto (Mario Baltali)
- Waldy's Pizza (Waldy Malouf)
- West Branch (Tom Valenti)
- 'wichcraft (Tom Colicchio)

VIETNAMESE

- Bôi
- Bün
- Doyers Viet.
- Nam
- Nha Trang
- Nicky's Viet.
- Omai
- Pho Bang
- Saigon Grill
- VietCafé

PRIX FIXE LUNCH FOR BELOW $30

Abboccato	$26	Mia Dona	24
Amalia	24	Milos	24
Anthos	28	Oceana	28
Artisinal	25	Olives	24
Asiate	24	Pampano	27
Capsouto Frères	24	Patroon	27
Five Points	20	Periyali	26
Fleur de Sel	29	Spice Market	17
I Trulli	24	Sushi Yasuda	23
Jean Georges	28	Tamarind	24
Kings' Carriage	19	Tao	24
Le Cirque	28	Tribeca Grill	29
Megu	29	Zarela	17

PRIX FIXE DINNER FOR $35 OR LESS

Becco	$23	La Mediterranée	35
B. Smith's	32	La Petite Auberge	29
Cafe Centro	35	Le Refuge	32
Café des Artistes	35	Maria Pia	23
Cafe Loup	28	Marseille	35
Chez Napoléon	30	Metrazur	35
Chin Chin	35	Notaro	27
Cibo	35	Sushi Yasuda	23
Compass	35	Tempo	32
Cornelia St. Cafe	25	Turkish Cuisine	27
Demarchelier	26	ViceVersa	35
etcetera etcetera	35	Village	29
Garden Cafe	32	Vong	35

PRE-THEATER DINNER FOR BELOW $30

Aki	$28	Gascogne	28
Alouette	25	Gavroche	20
Atlantic Grill	28	Jewel of India	28
Bay Leaf	21	Le Singe Vert	29
Bistro du Nord	20	Métisse	22
Brasserie Julien	25	Ocean Grill	25
Café de Bruxelles	25	Pascalou	20
Cascina	25	Pasha	24
Cebu	21	Savann	21
Dervish Turkish	28	Sharz Cafe	22

OTHER GOOD VALUES

Alice's Tea Cup | *American*
Bereket | *Turkish*
Better Burger | *Burgers*
Big Wong | *Chinese*
Brennan & Carr | *Sandwiches*
Cafe Cluny | *American/French*
Caracas | *Venezuelan*
Carl's | *Cheese Steaks*
Caviar Russe | *American*
Chop't Creative | *American*
Coals | *Pizza*
Congee | *Chinese*
Cubana Café | *Cuban*
Dishes | *Sandwiches*
Dumpling Man | *Chinese*
Empanada Mama | *S American*
Energy Kitchen | *Health Food*
Excellent Dumpling | *Chinese*
Felidia | *Italian*
goodburger | *Burgers*
Hale & Hearty | *Sandwiches/Soup*
Hampton Chutney | *Indian*
Hummus Place | *Israeli/Veg.*
Joe & Pat's | *Italian/Pizza*
Joe's Pizza | *Pizza*

Kittichai | *Thai*
L & B Spumoni | *Dessert/Pizza*
La Taza de Oro | *Diner*
Lenny's | *Sandwiches*
Mama's Food | *American*
McCormick & Schmick's | *Seafood*
Mill Korean | *Korean*
99 Miles to Philly | *Cheese Steaks*
Nyonya | *Malaysian*
Peanut Butter | *Sandwiches*
Penelope | *American*
Pepe | *Italian*
Pink Tea Cup | *Soul/Southern*
Pump Energy | *Health Food*
Quantum Leap | *Health/Veg.*
Rice | *Eclectic*
SEA | *Thai*
Thai Pavilion | *Thai*
Tia Pol | *Spanish*
Tierras | *Colombian*
Utsav | *Indian*
Veselka | *Ukrainian*
Vivolo | *Italian*
Wo Hop | *Chinese*

BEST OF THE BOROUGHS

Al Di La | *Brooklyn*
Baluchi's | *Queens*
Bamonte's | *Brooklyn*
Brennan & Carr | *Brooklyn*
Cebu | *Brooklyn*
Coals | *Bronx*
Coco Roco | *Brooklyn*
Cubana Café | *Brooklyn*
Denino's | *Staten Island*
Di Fara | *Brooklyn*
Diner | *Brooklyn*
Dominick's | *Bronx*
Don Peppe | *Queens*
DuMont | *Brooklyn*
East Manor | *Queens*
El Malecon | *Bronx*
Erawan | *Queens*
Fette Sau | *Brooklyn*
Fiorentino's | *Brooklyn*
Five Guys | *Brooklyn/Queens*
Franny's | *Brooklyn*
Garden Cafe | *Brooklyn*
Grand Sichuan | *Queens*
Grimaldi's | *Brooklyn/Queens*
Hale & Hearty | *Brooklyn*
Jackson Diner | *Queens*
Joe & Pat's | *Staten Island*
Joe's Pizza | *Brooklyn*
Joe's Shanghai | *Queens*
Joya | *Brooklyn*

Junior's | *Brooklyn*
Kum Gang San | *Queens*
La Flor | *Queens*
L&B Spumoni | *Brooklyn*
Leo's Latticini | *Queens*
Lucali | *Brooklyn*
Mill Basin | *Brooklyn*
Moim | *Brooklyn*
Nicky's | *Brooklyn*
Nyonya | *Brooklyn*
Patricia's | *Bronx*
Peter's | *Brooklyn*
Pho Bang | *Queens*
Ping's | *Queens*
Pio Pio | *Bronx/Queens*
Quantum Leap | *Queens*
Rice | *Brooklyn*
SEA | *Brooklyn*
Sette Enoteca | *Brooklyn*
67 Burger | *Brooklyn*
Smoke Joint | *Brooklyn*
Song | *Brooklyn*
Spicy & Tasty | *Queens*
Sripraphai | *Queens*
Sweet-n-Tart | *Queens*
Tempo | *Brooklyn*
Teresa's | *Brooklyn*
Thai Pavilion | *Queens*
Tierras Colombianas | *Queens*
Tom's | *Brooklyn*

RESTAURANT DIRECTORY

	FOOD	DECOR	SERVICE	COST

Abboccato *Italian*
21 | 19 | 20 | $62

W 50s | Blakely Hotel | 136 W. 55th St. (bet. 6th & 7th Aves.) | 212-265-4000 |
www.abboccato.com

"Interesting" Italian food, "lovely" digs and a "convenient" location
"across from City Center" add up to "delightful" dining at this "discreet"
Midtown sibling of Oceana and Molyvos; alright, it's "kinda pricey",
but its "wonderful" lunch/pre-theater prix fixes are good "value."

Adrienne's Pizzabar ● *Pizza*
24 | 16 | 15 | $24

Financial District | 87 Pearl St. (bet. Coenties Slip & Hanover Sq.) |
212-248-3838 | www.adriennespizzabar.com

"Addictive", "crispy" pies for "bargain" tabs draw hordes to this "happening" Financial District pizzeria that's a suits "zoo" at prime times;
"subpar" service and "nothing-special" decor are trumped by outdoor
seating that feels like a "movie set of old NY."

Aki *Japanese*
26 | 13 | 20 | $44

G Village | 181 W. Fourth St. (bet. Barrow & Jones Sts.) | 212-989-5440

"Tables fill early" at this "tiny", nondescript Village Japanese known
for "imaginative" sushi "beautifully presented" with "Caribbean flair";
devotees dub it a "Nobu-like experience on a small scale", enhanced
by "gracious service" and a "bargain" $28 pre-theater prix fixe.

Al Di La *Italian*
26 | 18 | 22 | $46

Park Slope | 248 Fifth Ave. (Carroll St.) | Brooklyn | 718-783-4565 |
www.aldilatrattoria.com

"Paradise" – save for the "no-reservations policy" – this "exceptional"
Park Slope Venetian is always "mobbed", so insiders "dine early or late
to avoid the crush", or cool their heels at the "cute" wine bar around
the corner; the cooking is "transcendent", the service "professional"
and the cost so much less than Manhattan that some surveyors are
"considering moving to Brooklyn."

Alice's Tea Cup *American*
19 | 20 | 17 | $25

E 60s | 156 E. 64th St. (Lexington Ave.) | 212-486-9200
E 80s | 220 E. 81st St. (bet. 2nd & 3rd Aves.) | 212-734-4832
W 70s | 102 W. 73rd St. (bet. Amsterdam & Columbus Aves.) | 212-799-3006
www.alicesteacup.com

A "fantasy world" for "ladies and little ladies", these "darling" tea-
rooms offer American finger sandwiches, "scrumptious scones" and

"giggly chitchat" over an "extravagant assortment" of cuppas; it may be a "madhouse" with "sluggish service" and "ridiculous waits", but ultimately it's "so cute you can't resist."

Alouette ● *French*

20 | 17 | 20 | $44

W 90s | 2588 Broadway (bet. 97th & 98th Sts.) | 212-222-6808 | www.alouettenyc.com

"Tiny and atmospheric", this "genteel" UWS "neighborhood standby" matches "classic *bonne femme*" French cooking with a "Left Bank" vibe and "welcoming" service; though tables are "tight", "decent" pricing and a $25 early-bird prix fixe "steal" seal the deal.

Amalia ⊠ *Mediterranean*

21 | 23 | 19 | $58

W 50s | 204 W. 55th St. (bet. B'way & 7th Ave.) | 212-245-1234 | www.amalia-nyc.com

"Flavorful" Mediterranean dishes compete with an "ornate", "urban cave" setting (think black-glass chandeliers, distressed brick walls) at this "stylish" Midtowner; "service could be better" and the pricing's "a tad high", but savvy sorts tout its bargain $24 lunch deal.

Amy's Bread *Bakery/Sandwiches*

23 | 11 | 16 | $13

Chelsea | Chelsea Mkt. | 75 Ninth Ave. (bet. 15th & 16th Sts.) | 212-462-4338
G Village | 250 Bleecker St. (bet. Carmine & Leroy Sts.) | 212-675-7802
W 40s | 672 Ninth Ave. (bet. 46th & 47th Sts.) | 212-977-2670
www.amysbread.com

Expect "long breadlines" at these bakery/sandwich shop/"carb heaven" combos where fans would "pay for the smell alone"; while the service is appropriately "flaky", "tight" setups make these "utilitarian" pit stops best for "takeout."

Anthos ⊠ *Greek*

24 | 20 | 21 | $69

W 50s | 36 W. 52nd St. (bet. 5th & 6th Aves.) | 212-582-6900 | www.anthosnyc.com

"Brilliant flavor combinations" underlie the "thrilling" menu of this "nouvelle Greek" "class operation" from chef Michael Psilakis and restauranteur Donatella Arpaia; it's already a "Midtown business standby" owing to the "adult" mood, "formal" service and "Aristotle Onassis"–worthy bills, though bargain seekers are hip to its $28 lunch special.

| | FOOD | DECOR | SERVICE | COST |

Arté Café *Italian*
| 18 | 17 | 16 | $36 |

W 70s | 106 W. 73rd St. (bet. Amsterdam & Columbus Aves.) |
212-501-7014 | www.artecafenyc.com

"Solid red-sauce" meals are the "staple" of this "serviceable" UWS
Italian, home to "good values", "hectic" service and a "lovely garden";
"lunch is quiet, dinner is not", and the $15.95 early-bird is a "bargain."

Artichoke Basille's Pizza ●⇄ *Pizza*
| 24 | 8 | 12 | $13 |

E Village | 328 E. 14th St. (bet. 1st & 2nd Aves.) | 212-228-2004

"Patience is a virtue" at this tiny new East Village slice joint that's
drawn "huge lines down the block" from day one thanks to a signature
"artichoke dip"-topped pie so "spectacular" that the "closet"-size di-
mensions and "snarky" service are forgotten; P.S. it's already notorious for keeping "crazy hours", so call ahead.

Artisanal *French*
| 23 | 20 | 20 | $54 |

Murray Hill | 2 Park Ave. (enter on 32nd St., bet. Madison & Park Aves.) |
212-725-8585 | www.artisanalbistro.com

A "mind-boggling mecca" for "cheese mavens", Terrance Brennan's
French brasserie in Murray Hill (aka "fondue heaven") also provides
"fairly priced" "comfort food à la français", "*charmant*" service and a
hard-to-beat $25 set-price lunch; regulars brush up on their "lip reading"
ahead of time since the "good-looking" space can be "cacophonous."

Asiate *American/Asian*
| 24 | 29 | 24 | $111 |

W 60s | Mandarin Oriental Hotel | 80 Columbus Circle, 35th fl.
(60th St. at B'way) | 212-805-8881 | www.mandarinoriental.com

"Dead-on" Central Park views and a room so "gorgeous" that it's rated
No. 1 for Decor add "wow" to this "tranquil haven" high in Columbus
Circle's Mandarin Oriental Hotel; new chef Toni Robertson offers a near
"flawless" menu of Asian–New American dishes, while "top-notch"
service adds to the "knockout" experience; true, the "splurge"-worthy
tabs are stunning in their own right, but the $24 prix fixe "lunch is a deal."

Atlantic Grill *Seafood*
| 23 | 19 | 20 | $53 |

E 70s | 1341 Third Ave. (bet. 76th & 77th Sts.) | 212-988-9200 |
www.brguestrestaurants.com

"So fresh you want to slap it", the "sure-bet" seafood at Steve Hanson's
UES "classic" continues to draw "teeming throngs" with "friendly" service and "almost reasonable" tabs (check out the $28 pre-theater spe-

	FOOD	DECOR	SERVICE	COST

cial); when the "festive" goings-on reach "rugby-scrum" proportions, regulars head for the "back room for conversation."

Baluchi's *Indian* — 17 | 13 | 15 | $27

E 50s | 224 E. 53rd St. (bet. 2nd & 3rd Aves.) | 212-750-5555
E 80s | 1724 Second Ave. (bet. 89th & 90th Sts.) | 212-996-2600
Gramercy | 329 Third Ave. (bet. 24th & 25th Sts.) | 212-679-3434
G Village | 361 Sixth Ave. (Washington Pl.) | 212-929-2441
G Village | 90 W. Third St. (bet. Sullivan & Thompson Sts.) | 212-529-5353
SoHo | 193 Spring St. (bet. Sullivan & Thompson Sts.) | 212-226-2828
TriBeCa | 275 Greenwich St. (Warren St.) | 212-571-5343
W 50s | 240 W. 56th St. (bet. B'way & 8th Ave.) | 212-397-0707
Forest Hills | 113-30 Queens Blvd. (bet. 76th Ave. & 76th Rd.) | Queens | 718-520-8600
www.baluchis.com

"Consistent if not outstanding", this "workmanlike", all-over-town Indian chain vends "solid", "generic" eats for "modest" sums; "dingy" decor and "below-par" service make them "better for takeout" – except at lunchtime, when the dine-in deal is "half-price."

Bamonte's *Italian* — 22 | 16 | 21 | $42

Williamsburg | 32 Withers St. (bet. Lorimer St. & Union Ave.) | Brooklyn | 718-384-8831

"When you're tired of hipsters", this vintage-1900 Williamsburg "trip back in time" is just the ticket for "delicious, old-world" Italian grub served by career waiters who've "been there forever"; maybe the "faded" decor "hasn't changed since day one", but the price is right at this "must-see" place.

Banjara ● *Indian* — 22 | 15 | 18 | $31

E Village | 97 First Ave. (6th St.) | 212-477-5956 | www.banjarany.com

"Much better than the run-of-the-mill Indians" on nearby Sixth Street, this "authentic" East Villager parlays "zesty, well-spiced" food that's worth every rupee; the staff is "pleasant", and even if the decor's "drab", at least there are "no Christmas lights."

Bar Boulud *French* — 22 | 20 | 20 | $63

W 60s | 1900 Broadway (bet. 63rd & 64th Sts.) | 212-595-0303 | www.danielnyc.com

Daniel Boulud goes "casual" at this new French wine bar facing Lincoln Center serving a rustic bistro menu topped off by a "much-vaunted" selection of charcuterie; as expected, the wine list is "excellent" and the pricing less than the chef's other venues, but the "simple" decor gets mixed marks ("wonderfully minimalist" vs. "upmarket tunnel").

Barney Greengrass 🅜🏷 *Deli*

| 24 | 7 | 14 | $27 |

W 80s | 541 Amsterdam Ave. (bet. 86th & 87th Sts.) | 212-724-4707 | www.barneygreengrass.com

"As good as NY deli gets" (and voted No. 1 in the genre), this 101-year-old UWS "shrine" to "Jewish soul food" reeks of "retro charm" with a "harried" mood and "deliciously dumpy" decor in need of a "schmear of paint"; though it's "cash only" and service is "as salty as the lox", the "smells alone are worth the price of admission."

bar Q *Pan-Asian*

| ∇ 20 | 18 | 21 | $53 |

W Village | 308-310 Bleecker St. (bet. Grove St. & 7th Ave. S.) | 212-206-7817 | www.barqrestaurant.com

Anita Lo's "distinctive" cooking has a new Village showcase at this "casual" Asian barbecue–cum–raw bar set in "minimalist", "stark white" digs with a greenhouse atrium; it's a bargain compared to her flagship.

Bay Leaf *Indian*

| 20 | 16 | 17 | $39 |

W 50s | 49 W. 56th St. (bet. 5th & 6th Aves.) | 212-957-1818 | www.bayleafnyc.com

At this "mellow" Indian near Carnegie Hall, you can count on "the classics", "economically priced" and served in "plentiful" portions by "solicitous" (if "slow") staffers; apart from white tablecloths, it's "no-frills", jazzed up by a "killer" $17 lunch buffet and a $21 pre-theater dinner.

Becco ◐ *Italian*

| 23 | 17 | 21 | $44 |

W 40s | 355 W. 46th St. (bet. 8th & 9th Aves.) | 212-397-7597 | www.becco-nyc.com

Simply a "sensation", Joe Bastianich's Restaurant Row Italian is famed for its all-the-carbs-you-can-eat $22.95 "pasta orgy" (accompanied by a "brilliant, $25-per-bottle wine list"); an "aim-to-please" staff ensures a "rollicking good time", no matter how "crowded" or "noisy" it gets.

Benoit *French*

| 18 | 20 | 16 | $69 |

W 50s | 60 W. 55th St. (bet. 5th & 6th Aves.) | 646-943-7373 | www.benoitny.com

Despite its pedigree as a spin-off of a wonderful old Parisian bistro and ownership by Alain Ducasse, this new Midtown eatery leaves surveyors, who expected a lot more than "just another French bistro", "disappointed"; still, it's a relatively affordable taste of Ducasse.

Bereket ●🍴 *Turkish* | 19 | 3 | 12 | $12 |

LES | 187 E. Houston St. (Orchard St.) | 212-475-7700
"Everything seems delicious after a night of drinking", and this 24/7 LES "snack king" is renowned as a place "where the cabbies go" for "cheap, fast" Turkish eats; ok, "not a dime was spent on decor", but it's still an "excellent late-night" pit stop.

Better Burger *Burgers* | 15 | 9 | 13 | $14 |

Chelsea | 178 Eighth Ave. (19th St.) | 212-989-6688 ●
Murray Hill | 561 Third Ave. (37th St.) | 212-949-7528
W 40s | 587 Ninth Ave. (bet. 42nd & 43rd Sts.) | 212-629-6622
www.betterburgernyc.com
"Fast food without the guilt" sums up the appeal of this "virtuous" mini-chain serving "organic burgers" and air-baked fries in "bright", "plain" settings; but those who think it "doesn't live up to its name" find the goods "underwhelming in flavor and above-average in cost", yet "better than a sharp stick in the eye."

Big Wong 🍴 *Chinese* | 22 | 5 | 11 | $14 |

Chinatown | 67 Mott St. (bet. Bayard & Canal Sts.) | 212-964-0540
"Cheap Chinese chow" arrives "piping hot" at "unbeatable" rates at this unfortunately named, "around-forever" relic of Chinatown; despite the "mayhem", "Formica" and "service with a grunt", it's "so worth it", especially when the yen for "delicious barbecue" and "genuine" congee hits.

Bistro du Nord *French* | 18 | 15 | 16 | $45 |

E 90s | 1312 Madison Ave. (93rd St.) | 212-289-0997
A "touch of Paree" lands in Carnegie Hill via this "quaint" French boîte known for its "fine" bistro standards and "terrific" prix fixes; its negatives include "bumper-to-bumper tables", an "awkward" duplex setting and "indifferent" service – yet locals are still "glad to have it."

Blaue Gans ● *Austrian/German* | 21 | 18 | 19 | $47 |

TriBeCa | 139 Duane St. (bet. Church St. & W. B'way) | 212-571-8880 |
www.wallse.com
"Sublime schnitzel" highlights the menu of this "casual" TriBeCa establishment where chef Kurt Gutenbrunner offers "delectable",

"affordable" takes on Austro-German cooking; the "low-tech, low-stress" setting emits an "intellectual" vibe, ditto the "polite", if somewhat "distracted", staff.

BLT Burger *Burgers*
19 | 14 | 16 | $25

G Village | 470 Sixth Ave. (bet. 11th & 12th Sts.) | 212-243-8226 | www.bltburger.com

The "BLT empire's bargain branch", this "fun" if "frenetic" Villager showcases Laurent Tourondel's "innovative" spins on "upscale" burgers, fries and "boozy shakes"; it may "fall short" in the service and decor departments, but few mind since the "price is right."

Blue Smoke *BBQ*
21 | 17 | 19 | $42

Gramercy | 116 E. 27th St. (bet. Lexington Ave. & Park Ave. S.) | 212-447-7733 | www.bluesmoke.com

It's permissable to "lick your fingers" at Danny Meyer's "civilized" Gramercy barbecue "mecca", turning out "serious", "falling-off-the-bone" ribs, "excellent beers" and "fab sides" in a bustling setting; while a few protest its "high-end lowbrow" dichotomy, there's agreement that the sounds from the downstairs Jazz Standard will "heal your soul."

Bôi *Vietnamese*
19 | 14 | 17 | $28

E 40s | 246 E. 44th St. (bet. 2nd & 3rd Aves.) | 212-681-6541

Bôi to Go ☒✄ *Vietnamese*

E 40s | 800 Second Ave. (bet. 42nd & 43rd Sts.) | 212-681-1122 | www.boi-restaurant.com

A "cool alternative" near Grand Central, this "upscale" but "low-key" Vietnamese vends "fresh", "spicy" dishes and "fabulous" desserts in "dark", "unobtrusive" digs; its nearby take-out site offers a "limited menu" of "quick-bite" sandwiches, all at "decent" prices.

Bouchon Bakery *American/French*
23 | 14 | 17 | $29

W 60s | Time Warner Ctr. | 10 Columbus Circle, 3rd fl. (60th St. at B'way) | 212-823-9366 | www.bouchonbakery.com

For a "decadent" shopping break, Thomas Keller's New American cafe/patisserie in the Time Warner Center injects a bit of "food heaven into everyday life" with its "sophisticated sandwiches" and "sublime" French pastries; despite the "food court" feel and "inconsistent" service, its "pedigree is obvious."

		FOOD	DECOR	SERVICE	COST

Brasserie Julien French
18 | 19 | 17 | $45

E 80s | 1422 Third Ave. (bet. 80th & 81st Sts.) | 212-744-6327 | www.brasseriejulien.com

Bringing "France" to Yorkville, this "charming" brasserie offers "solid" Gallic grub in "congenial" deco digs, where the "Parisian flair" extends to the "uneven service"; insiders say it's best experienced on weekends when there's "live jazz", but it's "*très enjoyable*" any day of the week.

Brennan & Carr ● ⊅ Sandwiches
20 | 8 | 15 | $17

Sheepshead Bay | 3432 Nostrand Ave. (Ave. U) | Brooklyn | 718-646-9559

"Nothing changes" at this "decades-old" Sheepshead Bay "blue-collar" landmark famed for its "messy" roast beef sandwiches "double-dipped" in au jus; the "same low prices" compensate for the "mediocre service" and "Dark Ages" decor.

brgr Burgers
18 | 13 | 14 | $16

Chelsea | 287 Seventh Ave. (bet. 26th & 27th Sts.) | 212-488-7500 | www.brgr.us

"Have it your way" at this Chelsea eatery where "build-it-yourself" burgers are "made to order" from "juicy" beef, turkey and veggie patties; though the "cafeteria-counter service" draws some fire, the "Fresca on tap" is simply "priceless."

Brooklyn Diner USA ● Diner
17 | 14 | 15 | $31

W 40s | 155 W. 43rd St. (bet. B'way & 6th Ave.) | 212-265-5400
W 50s | 212 W. 57th St. (bet. B'way & 7th Ave.) | 212-977-2280
www.brooklyndiner.com

"Hefty portions" of "elevated diner" food at affordable prices draw "animated" crowds to these "fast-paced" American "throwbacks" from Shelly Fireman; despite "theme-park decor" and "preoccupied" staffers, they're "well located" and you certainly "won't leave hungry."

B. Smith's Restaurant Row Southern
18 | 19 | 19 | $47

W 40s | 320 W. 46th St. (bet. 8th & 9th Aves.) | 212-315-1100 | www.bsmith.com

A "solid" pre-theater choice, this "cheerful" Restaurant Row "standby" serves midpriced, "stick-to-your-ribs" Southern grub in an "earthy, welcoming" room (plus a bargain $32 dinner prix fixe); customers "love it", especially when charming TV celeb/owner Barbara Smith is around.

	FOOD	DECOR	SERVICE	COST

Bukhara Grill *Indian* | 22 | 16 | 19 | $36 |

E 40s | 217 E. 49th St. (bet. 2nd & 3rd Aves.) | 212-888-2839 | www.bukharany.com

The $16.95 lunch buffet is a "reasonably priced" "spice delight" at this U.N.-area Indian that curries favor with "tasty" vittles and "calm" atmospherics; maybe the "interior could use an upgrade", but the small second-floor terrace is fine as is.

Bún ● *Vietnamese* | ▽ 21 | 17 | 18 | $31 |

SoHo | 143 Grand St. (bet. Crosby & Lafayette Sts.) | 212-431-7999 | www.eatbun.com

"High-concept creations" at "great prices" lure fans to this "innovative" new 24/7 SoHo Vietnamese where the "flavorful" namesake staple (rice vermicelli) appears in many forms on the menu; too bad the "modern", stylishly spare decor seems at odds with the "clunky" service.

burger joint at | 23 | 9 | 11 | $15 |
Le Parker Meridien ●⊅ *Burgers*

W 50s | Le Parker Meridien | 119 W. 56th St. (bet. 6th & 7th Aves.) | 212-708-7414 | www.parkermeridien.com

For "top-class burgers" in the "most unlikely" setting, check out this "old-school" hamburger joint incongruously "tucked away behind a curtain" in a "swank" Midtown hotel lobby; while the chow scores well, the "intimidating service", "lowbrow decor", "minimal seating" and "unbearable" lunch lines don't; P.S. the secret's out, "even Oprah knows."

Cafe Centro ⊠ *Mediterranean* | 19 | 18 | 19 | $48 |

E 40s | MetLife Bldg. | 200 Park Ave. (45th St.) | 212-818-1222 | www.patinagroup.com

The "classic business lunch" is in full swing at this "vibrant" brasserie near Grand Central that lures throngs with "dependable" Med meals, "efficient" service and "commuter convenience"; those seeking "more relaxed", crowd-free dining report that the $35 prix fixe "dinner is a delight."

Cafe Cluny ● *American/French* | 20 | 19 | 19 | $49 |

W Village | 284 W. 12th St. (W. 4th St.) | 212-255-6900 | www.cafecluny.com

Popular with "wafer-thin" models and "arty celebs", this "sunny", "sceney" Village bistro serves a "simple but delicious" French-American menu; devotees report this "instant classic" is especially "popular" (read: "cramped") for brunch; N.B. don't miss its $30 pre-theater dinner deal.

Café de Bruxelles ◗ *Belgian* | 20 | 15 | 19 | $42 |

W Village | 118 Greenwich Ave. (13th St.) | 212-206-1830

"There's more to the menu than moules frites" at this "venerable" West Villager that also offers seldom-seen "Belgian favorites" and an "extensive selection" of Trappist beer; prices are "modest" and service "relaxed", so despite the "stodgy" feel, most report "life is good" here.

Café des Artistes ◗ *French* | 22 | 26 | 23 | $69 |

W 60s | 1 W. 67th St. (bet. Columbus Ave. & CPW) | 212-877-3500 | www.cafenyc.com

The "older the violin, the sweeter the music" says it all about this "classy" UWS "grande dame" via George and Jenifer Lang that "still seduces" with an "oh-so-romantic setting" that combines "beautiful flowers" and "sensual murals" of wood nymphs with "delicious" French dishes and "excellent service"; a "feast for the eyes and palate", it's "quintessential NYC" and worth every penny; N.B. for a less expensive alternative, check out their $35 prix fixe dinner menu.

Café Evergreen *Chinese* | 20 | 12 | 19 | $32 |

E 60s | 1288 First Ave. (bet. 69th & 70th Sts.) | 212-744-3266

"Who needs Chinatown?" when there's this "reliably good" UES Cantonese serving some of the "best dim sum north of Canal" backed up by an "amazing wine list" and "understanding" service; maybe the decor's "uninspired", but the pricing's "reasonable" and "delivery is fast."

Cafe Loup ◗ *French* | 19 | 17 | 19 | $43 |

G Village | 105 W. 13th St. (bet. 6th Ave. & 7th Ave. S.) | 212-255-4746

"Your favorite pair of shoes in restaurant form", this "steady" French bistro brings "a bit of the Left Bank to the Village" via its "grown-up atmosphere", "not fussy" traditional menu and "easily digestible bills."

Capsouto Frères *French* | 23 | 22 | 23 | $57 |

TriBeCa | 451 Washington St. (Watts St.) | 212-966-4900 | www.capsoutofreres.com

"Bring your GPS" – this "middle-of-nowhere" TriBeCa "mainstay" is "worth seeking out" for "classic" French bistro fare (including "sublime" soufflés) and a well priced $24 lunch prix fixe; "friendly" staffers preside over a "quiet", "beautifully unstuffy room" that manages to be "cozy despite the high ceilings"; thankfully, there's easy parking.

Caracas Arepa Bar *Venezuelan*

25 | 13 | 16 | $19

E Village | 93½ E. Seventh St. (bet. Ave. A & 1st Ave.) | 212-529-2314

Caracas to Go *Venezuelan*

E Village | 91 E. Seventh St. (1st Ave.) | 212-228-5062
www.caracasarepabar.com

"Creative gourmet riffs" on "unusual" stuffed arepas are a "steal" at this "tiny sliver of Venezuela" in the East Village; since service runs on "South American time" and there's often a "long wait", try takeout next door for a "cheap", "filling" fix.

Carl's Steaks *Cheese Steaks*

21 | 5 | 12 | $13

Murray Hill | 507 Third Ave. (34th St.) | 212-696-5336 ●
TriBeCa | 79 Chambers St. (bet. B'way & Church St.) | 212-566-2828
www.carlssteaks.com

"Yo, Philly fans", this Murray Hill–TriBeCa duo dishes out "cheap", "sloppy" cheese steaks smothered in Cheez Whiz that are as close to "authentic" "as you'll find in NYC"; since there's not much service, decor or seating, either "eat standing up" or get it to go.

Carmine's *Italian*

20 | 15 | 18 | $40

W 40s | 200 W. 44th St. (bet. B'way & 8th Ave.) | 212-221-3800 ●
W 90s | 2450 Broadway (bet. 90th & 91st Sts.) | 212-362-2200
www.carminesnyc.com

The "more the merrier" could be the motto of these "jumping" West Side eatfests where "gargantuan", family-style portions of "budget"-priced Southern Italian grub can feed "an army"; it's "always fun" and always "packed" despite "choppy service", "long waits" and "tourist throngs"; just "bring your family and friends" and "come hungry."

Carnegie Deli ●⊄ *Deli*

21 | 9 | 13 | $28

W 50s | 854 Seventh Ave. (55th St.) | 212-757-2245 | www.carnegiedeli.com

For "sandwiches piled to the ceiling" and "marvelous cheesecake", check out this "NY classic" (circa 1937) Midtown deli; decor is "sparse", service "wiseacre" and payment cash-only, but that doesn't keep "tourists", "natives" and *Broadway Danny Rose* fans from squeezing in to those long communal tables for what may be "too much of a good thing" – "oy vey."

	FOOD	DECOR	SERVICE	COST

Cascina ● *Italian* — 19 | 16 | 18 | $40

W 40s | 647 Ninth Ave. (bet. 45th & 46th Sts.) | 212-245-4422 | www.cascina.com

With "homey food" and an "unassuming" attitude, this "safe-bet" Hell's Kitchen Italian "knows what it is" – a "handy" choice for locals and theatergoers seeking "good value"; a "wood-burning stove" and wines from their own vineyard add to the experience.

Caviar Russe *American* — 24 | 22 | 22 | $95

E 50s | 538 Madison Ave., 2nd fl. (bet. 54th & 55th Sts.) | 212-980-5908 | www.caviarrusse.com

Vending a "perfect marriage of caviar and sushi", this "grown-up" Midtown American offers "sublime" dining in a "casually elegant" room overseen by "pro" staffers; sure, it's "expensive" and the mezzanine location "quirky", but the $30 pre-theater prix fixe is hard to beat for "sophisticated" supping.

Cebu ● *Continental* — 21 | 19 | 19 | $38

Bay Ridge | 8801 Third Ave. (88th St.) | Brooklyn | 718-492-5095

Bay Ridge's "first choice" for "late-night" dining (till 3 AM), this "always crowded" Continental purveys a "tasty", midpriced menu that's especially "delicious" for weekend brunch; regulars eschew the "din at the bar", head for the "intimate" back room and dig into the $21 pre-theater dinner.

Chef Ho's Peking Duck Grill *Chinese* — 22 | 13 | 18 | $30

E 80s | 1720 Second Ave. (bet. 89th & 90th Sts.) | 212-348-9444

The "name says it all" at this "semi-upscale" UES Chinese where the "fantastic" signature dish is "as good as Chinatown" and the tabs are "bargain" priced; even if the atmosphere's "ordinary", the "accommodating" staff makes sure the "welcome is warm."

Chennai Garden *Indian/Vegetarian* — 22 | 10 | 14 | $23

Gramercy | 129 E. 27th St. (Park Ave. S.) | 212-689-1999

"Solid vegetarian" food that's "kosher to boot" is yours at this "tasty" Gramercy Parker where the "spicy" South Indian specialties come out "quick and easy" (not to mention "cheaply"); though there's "not much decor", the $6.95 all-you-can-eat lunch buffet more than compensates.

	FOOD	DECOR	SERVICE	COST

Chez Napoléon ⊠ *French* | 21 | 15 | 21 | $45 |

W 50s | 365 W. 50th St. (bet. 8th & 9th Aves.) | 212-265-6980 |
www.cheznapoleon.com

Sure, it's a real "throwback", but "that's the attraction" at this circa-1960
Theater District "old-timer" whose French cooking is more *grand-mère* than haute; though it could stand some "refurbishing", the "reasonable" pricing and "family-owned" feeling are fine as is.

ChikaLicious *Dessert* | 25 | 17 | 22 | $23 |

E Village | 203 E. 10th St. (bet. 1st & 2nd Aves.) | 212-995-9511 |
E Village | 204 E. 10th St. (bet. 1st & 2nd Aves.) | 212-475-0929 ◑
www.chikalicious.com

"Delectable desserts" are the thing at this "pint-size" East Village
sweet specialist offering three-course prix fixes along with optional
wine pairings; although a few feel it's a bit "pricey for the portion size",
the "long lines" out front speak for themselves; N.B. the new across-
the-street offshoot doing takeout only may help curtail the queues.

Chin Chin ◑ *Chinese* | 23 | 18 | 21 | $51 |

E 40s | 216 E. 49th St. (bet. 2nd & 3rd Aves.) | 212-888-4555 |
www.chinchinny.com

For a taste of "emperor's dining", this longtime Midtown Chinese offers
"delicate, satisfying" dishes including a "must-try" Grand Marnier
shrimp; its "corporate" following feels it's "worth the premium" prices
given such "refined" fare and "courteous" service, while regular folk
show up for the bargain-priced $35 dinner prix fixe.

Cho Dang Gol *Korean* | 23 | 15 | 17 | $29 |

Garment District | 55 W. 35th St. (bet. 5th & 6th Aves.) | 212-695-8222 |
www.chodanggolny.com

The "signature tofu dishes are a must" at this "authentic" Garment
District Korean popular with "young" expats lured in by "cleanly prepared" dishes that are "good for your taste buds and your soul"; the
"value" pricing is pretty "comforting" too.

Chola *Indian* | 23 | 16 | 20 | $37 |

E 50s | 232 E. 58th St. (bet. 2nd & 3rd Aves.) | 212-688-4619 |
www.fineindiandining.com

"Pitch-perfect" Indian cuisine mixing the "traditional" with "offbeat
regional" dishes awaits at this "adventurous" Eastsider that dares to

go "beyond tikka masala"; while the "variety" and "knowledgeable" service earn kudos, it's the "superb" \$13.95 lunch buffet that's most applause-worthy.

Chop't Creative Salad *American*

	FOOD	DECOR	SERVICE	COST
	19	9	13	\$13

E 50s | 165 E. 52nd St. (bet. Lexington & 3rd Aves.) | 212-421-2300 🔂

E 50s | 60 E. 56th St. (bet. Madison & Park Aves.) | 212-750-2467 🔂

Union Sq | 24 E. 17th St. (bet. B'way & 5th Ave.) | 646-336-5523

W 50s | 145 W. 51st St. (bet. 6th & 7th Aves.) | 212-974-8140 🔂

www.choptsalad.com

Lettuce lovers can't resist the "siren song" of these "efficient", modern salad shops that crank out "custom" combos of "amazingly fresh" greens and toppings; "insane" lunchtime lines and "pricey" tabs for the genre come with the territory.

Cibo *American/Italian*

	FOOD	DECOR	SERVICE	COST
	19	17	20	\$46

E 40s | 767 Second Ave. (41st St.) | 212-681-1616

"Comfortable" and "accommodating", this Tuscan–New American offers "hearty servings" of midpriced, reliably good food ferried by an "attentive" crew; proximity to Grand Central Station makes it a "fine fallback" for "relaxed business lunching", and the \$35 dinner prix fixe is just as calming.

City Bakery *Bakery*

	FOOD	DECOR	SERVICE	COST
	21	11	12	\$19

Flatiron | 3 W. 18th St. (bet. 5th & 6th Aves.) | 212-366-1414 | www.thecitybakery.com

Though its "distinctive" salad bar/buffet is "always fresh", Maury Rubin's Flatiron "staple" is best known for its "superlative" baked goods and "addictive hot chocolate" for a fair price; so even if the "search for a seat" can be difficult, word is you "can't go wrong" here.

Clinton St. Baking Co. *American*

	FOOD	DECOR	SERVICE	COST
	25	13	16	\$27

LES | 4 Clinton St. (bet. Houston & Stanton Sts.) | 646-602-6263 | www.greatbiscuits.com

It's worth braving the "looong" lines for "pancakes from Cloud Nine" at this exceptional LES American bakery/cafe justifiably renowned for its "killer" weekend brunch; it's so "small" that "only the slim may dine comfortably", though access is easier at the calmer dinner hour.

	FOOD	DECOR	SERVICE	COST

Coals ☒ *Pizza*
∇ 23 | 15 | 17 | $21

Bronx | 1888 Eastchester Rd. (Morris Park Ave.) | 718-823-7002 | www.coalspizza.com

Distinguished by its "novel" concept – "irresistible" *grilled* pizzas – this "unique" Bronx joint also offers a "limited", "inexpensive" selection of soup, salad and panini; "friendly" service and a "youthful vibe" keep it popular with "mainly locals"; N.B. closed weekends.

Coco Roco *Peruvian*
21 | 14 | 15 | $26

Cobble Hill | 139 Smith St. (bet. Bergen & Dean Sts.) | Brooklyn | 718-254-9933

Park Slope | 392 Fifth Ave. (bet. 6th & 7th Sts.) | Brooklyn | 718-965-3376

There's "a lot happening on the plate" at these "festive" Brooklyn Peruvians where "little coin" buys "plentiful" portions and an especially "heavenly" rotisserie chicken; "slow" service and not much decor don't hamper the "hopping" scene.

Comfort Diner *Diner*
16 | 11 | 15 | $21

E 40s | 214 E. 45th St. (bet. 2nd & 3rd Aves.) | 212-867-4555

Flatiron | 25 W. 23rd St. (bet. 5th & 6th Aves.) | 212-741-1010 www.comfortdiner.com

It's "Thanksgiving every day" at this "old-timey", "just-what-the-name-says" duo-slinging "better-than-average diner food" that "sticks to your ribs" but won't empty your wallet; too bad the "indifferent service" and "tired" "'50s-style" decor make some uncomfortable.

Compass *American*
22 | 23 | 21 | $59

W 70s | 208 W. 70th St. (bet. Amsterdam & West End Aves.) | 212-875-8600 | www.compassrestaurant.com

"Civil acoustics" permit "quiet conversation" at this "comfortable" UWS New American that hits "all the right points" with "first-rate" food and "beautiful" looks; tabs tend to skew up, but on Sundays the "tremendous" wine list is half-price, an "amazing deal", and there's a $35 dinner prix fixe.

Congee ❶ *Chinese*
20 | 13 | 13 | $22

Little Italy | 98 Bowery (bet. Grand & Hester Sts.) | 212-965-5028

Congee Bowery ❶ *Chinese*
LES | 207 Bowery (bet. Rivington & Spring Sts.) | 212-766-2828

(continued)

Congee Village ◐ *Chinese*

LES | 100 Allen St. (bet. Broome & Delancey Sts.) | 212-941-1818 | www.congeevillagerestaurants.com

You can "eat till you drop" for "super-value" prices at these separately owned Downtown Cantonese specializing in the eponymous rice porridge that's the equivalent of "Chinese chicken soup"; all locations sport "kitschy" decor, but Congee Village looks like a "set from *Indiana Jones and the Temple of Doom.*"

Cornelia Street Cafe ◐ *American/French* `19` `16` `18` `$35`

G Village | 29 Cornelia St. (bet. Bleecker & W. 4th Sts.) | 212-989-9319 | www.corneliastreetcafe.com

It doesn't get more "Village-y" than this French-American "old friend", dishing out "home-cooked meals" and "fantastic brunches" since 1977; "decent prices", "cool vibes" and eclectic entertainment in its downstairs space have made it a bona fide neighborhood "haunt."

Corner Bistro ◐⇻ *Burgers* `22` `9` `12` `$16`

W Village | 331 W. Fourth St. (Jane St.) | 212-242-9502

"Grimy" decor is "part of the charm" at this "genuine" Village tavern famed for its "thick", "messy" burgers, "paper-plate" china and "dirt-cheap beer"; expect "long lines" of "frat boys" with "impending hangovers" who don't mind the "military service" or "truck stop restrooms."

Crispo ◐ *Italian* `23` `19` `20` `$47`

W Village | 240 W. 14th St. (bet. 7th & 8th Aves.) | 212-229-1818 | www.crisporestaurant.com

"Popularity has led to crowds" at this "former hidden gem" in the West Village offering "honest" Northern Italian cooking for "affordable" rates; "cozy" digs, "attentive" service and a "magical", all-seasons garden add up to "reliably good" dining.

Cubana Café ◐⇻ *Cuban* `19` `15` `15` `$23`

G Village | 110 Thompson St. (bet. Prince & Spring Sts.) | 212-966-5366
Carroll Gardens | 272 Smith St. (bet. Degraw & Sackett Sts.) | Brooklyn | 718-858-3980

"Hearty" Cuban eats for "inexpensive" dough keep this "folksy" Village-Carroll Gardens duo popular with a "cool young crowd"; "ridiculously small" settings, a "cash-only" policy and "iffy" service are downsides.

	FOOD	DECOR	SERVICE	COST

Da Andrea *Italian*

23 | 14 | 21 | $36

W Village | 557 Hudson St. (bet. Perry & W. 11th Sts.) | 212-367-1979 | www.biassanot.com

"Narrow on space but broad in appeal", this longtime West Village Italian boasts "flavorful" Emilia-Romagna "home cooking" served by an "easygoing" crew that treats patrons "like family"; though "not much on looks", few notice given the "low prices" and "happy" mood.

Daisy May's BBQ USA *BBQ*

22 | 6 | 12 | $23

W 40s | 623 11th Ave. (46th St.) | 212-977-1500 | www.daisymaysbbq.com

Hog-wild fans of this "no-frills", cafeteria-style smoke hut in Hell's Kitchen "hunker down" at "communal" picnic tables over "succulent ribs" and other "knockout" BBQ, bolstered by "right tasty" fixin's, all at tabs that Li'l Abner could afford; a Midtown satellite lunch cart saves admirers the "trek" to the Way West Side.

Dawat *Indian*

23 | 18 | 20 | $49

E 50s | 210 E. 58th St. (bet. 2nd & 3rd Aves.) | 212-355-7555

Long a "best bet" for "gourmet Indian" dining, this East Midtowner showcases actress/chef Madhur Jaffrey's "blissful" takes on classic dishes, abetted by "fine service" and a "soothing" ambiance; even though some say the "bloom is off" the somewhat "staid" surroundings, it's still "worth every rupee."

Demarchelier *French*

17 | 15 | 16 | $47

E 80s | 50 E. 86th St. (bet. Madison & Park Aves.) | 212-249-6300 | www.demarchelierrestaurant.com

Upper Eastsiders make this "relaxed" French bistro a "hopping hangout" for "solid" comfort food and "active bar" scenery at prices that are "*très raisonnables*" for the neighborhood; though cynics nix the "plain setting", "tight tables" and "snooty staff", regulars say that's what makes it "authentic."

Denino's Pizzeria ⊅ *Pizza*

25 | 10 | 17 | $20

Staten Island | 524 Port Richmond Ave. (bet. Hooker Pl. & Walker St.) | 718-442-9401

A Staten Island mainstay since 1937, this "old-time" pizza parlor plies "addictive" thin-crust pies washed down with "cheap beer"; the "bare-bones" decor and "family atmospherics" may "leave plenty to be desired", but "be prepared to fight crowds on weekends" all the same.

	FOOD	DECOR	SERVICE	COST

Dervish Turkish ● *Turkish* `19` `15` `18` `$36`

W 40s | 146 W. 47th St. (bet. 6th & 7th Aves.) | 212-997-0070 |
www.dervishrestaurant.com

"Something different" in the Theater District, this "handy" Turk offers
"tasty" standards and "swift service" that will whirl you out "before
the curtain goes up"; the bi-level space could stand a "makeover", but
most focus on the "affordable" cost, notably that $28 early-bird dinner.

Di Fara Ⓜ⇗ *Pizza* `27` `4` `8` `$14`

Midwood | 1424 Ave. J (bet. 14th & 15th Sts.) | Brooklyn | 718-258-1367 |
www.difara.com

"Di-licious" is the word on this Midwood "Holy Grail of pizza", a circa-
1963 "hole-in-the-wall" where "master" chef Dominic De Marco re-
wards "insane waits" with "sublime" "handcrafted" pies; sure, it's
"four bucks a slice", but admirers aver "there's no better on the planet."

Dim Sum Go Go *Chinese* `21` `12` `14` `$22`

Chinatown | 5 E. Broadway (Chatham Sq.) | 212-732-0797

"Nontraditional" dim sum "prepared to order" and served all day
means "no carts" and "less chaos" at this Chinatown novelty; purists
protest "it's not the same experience" sans trolleys and nix the "sterile
decor" but admit the "tranquil" mood is a "relief."

Diner ● *Diner* `21` `17` `17` `$33`

Williamsburg | 85 Broadway (Berry St.) | Brooklyn | 718-486-3077 |
www.dinernyc.com

"Cool but approachable", this "offbeat" South Williamsburg "favorite" lures "hipsters" with "homespun", well-priced New American
diner chow served by "tattooed girls" in a "funky", "pre-war" dining
car; just "be prepared to wait" on weekends, when "brunch is what
it's all about."

Dinosaur Bar-B-Que *BBQ* `22` `16` `17` `$29`

Harlem | 646 W. 131st St. (12th Ave.) | 212-694-1777 |
www.dinosaurbarbque.com

"Yabba dabba doo"-size portions of "bodacious", "butt-kicking BBQ"
chased with "awesome" microbrews keep this "rollicking" West
Harlem honky-tonk "crazy busy" with curious 'cue connoisseurs cag-
ing a "real-deal bargain"; just make sure to "have a reservation" to
avoid the "mad scramble to get a seat."

	FOOD	DECOR	SERVICE	COST

Dirty Bird to-go *American* | 19 | 6 | 14 | $16 |

W Village | 204 W. 14th St. (7th Ave.) | 212-620-4836 |
www.dirtybirdtogo.com

"Urban picnic" types say this West Village "takeaway" specialist is their
"go-to" for "delish" fried and rotisserie versions of "free-range chicken"
paired with "down-home sides", all for a good price; it's a "worthwhile"
fast-food "alternative", though some cluck about the "portion size."

Dishes *Sandwiches* | 21 | 12 | 11 | $17 |

E 40s | 6 E. 45th St. (bet. 5th & Madison Aves.) | 212-687-5511 🖪
E 40s | Grand Central | lower level (42nd St. & Vanderbilt Ave.) |
212-808-5511
E 50s | Citigroup Ctr. | 399 Park Ave. (53rd St.) | 212-421-5511 🖪

"Wildly popular" with Midtown's "upwardly mobile" nine-to-fivers,
this threesome's "mouthwatering array" of "high-class" sandwiches,
soups and salads attracts "madhouse hordes" at lunch; but as ratings
show, decor and service aren't their strong suit.

Do Hwa *Korean* | ▽ 21 | 17 | 18 | $38 |

G Village | 55 Carmine St. (Bedford St.) | 212-414-1224 |
www.dohwanyc.com

As "close to authentic" as Korean food gets in the Village, this "flavorful" BBQ specialist puts out "tasty" chow at "K-town comparable"
prices in a "chic", "modern-ish" setting; "interactive" types say it's
even more "fun" if you "sizzle your own" at a grill table.

Dok Suni's ●☞ *Korean* | ▽ 22 | 13 | 17 | $34 |

E Village | 119 First Ave. (bet. St. Marks Pl. & 7th St.) | 212-477-9506

"Downtown types" dock at this "cash-only" East Villager for "kickin'"
"Korean comfort food" that "fills you up without breaking the bank";
"excellent" cocktails ratchet up the "lively" vibe, even if the space
"needs more seating" and decor.

Dominick's ☞ *Italian* | 23 | 10 | 17 | $38 |

Bronx | 2335 Arthur Ave. (bet. Crescent Ave. & E. 187th St.) | 718-733-2807

"Nobody goes home hungry" from this "legendary", cash-only Bronx
Italian where "scrumptious" cooking is served at shared tables with
"no menu" ("just ask what's good") and "no check" (they'll "tell you
what you owe"); the "decor's better" following a recent renovation,
but the no-reservations policy means the same "crazy-long waits."

	FOOD	DECOR	SERVICE	COST

Don Peppe Ⓜ✄ *Italian* | 25 | 10 | 18 | $44 |

Ozone Park | 135-58 Lefferts Blvd. (bet. 135th & 149th Aves.) | Queens | 718-845-7587

Garlic lovers relish the "superior red-sauce" Italiana plated at this Ozone Park "institution" where the "enormous", "family-style" portions are washed down with "homemade wine"; "wear loose clothes", "bring cash" (they don't take plastic) and be prepared for "no frills."

Doyers Vietnamese *Vietnamese* | ▽ 21 | 4 | 13 | $18 |

Chinatown | 11-13 Doyers St., downstairs (Chatham Sq.) | 212-513-1521

The Chinatown basement locale may be "hard to find", but this "windowless dive" is one of the "best Vietnamese bargains" around; "somnambulant service" and "zero ambiance" are reflected in the rock-bottom pricing.

DuMont *American* | 24 | 17 | 18 | $27 |

Williamsburg | 432 Union Ave. (bet. Devoe St. & Metropolitan Ave.) | Brooklyn | 718-486-7717 | www.dumontrestaurant.com

DuMont Burger ● *American*

Williamsburg | 314 Bedford Ave. (bet. S. 1st & 2nd Sts.) | Brooklyn | 718-384-6127 | www.dumontnyc.com

Williamsburgers can "stop cooking at home" thanks to this "easygoing joint" serving "artful" yet "cheap" New American standards; a "hip crowd" convenes in the "inviting" interior or "Zen-like garden", or hits the Bedford Avenue mini spin-off for "awesome" burgers and sandwiches.

Dumpling Man ● *Chinese* | 18 | 7 | 12 | $12 |

E Village | 100 St. Marks Pl. (bet. Ave. A & 1st Ave.) | 212-505-2121 | www.dumplingman.com

When it comes to a "cheap" quickie, this "painless" East Village Chinese offers "lots to choose from" via a "flavorful" roster of "substantial dumplings", all "freshly made" right in front of you; but given the "hole-in-the-wall" setting, "takeout is the best bet."

East Manor *Chinese* | 19 | 12 | 12 | $25 |

Flushing | 46-45 Kissena Blvd. (bet. Kalmia & Laburnum Aves.) | Queens | 718-888-8998 | www.eastmanor.us

"Hong Kong-style" carts provide "lots of selection" at this "huge" Flushing Chinese that specializes in "tantalizing" dim sum at lunchtime and on weekends; low prices and "fast (if not friendly)" service keep things "bustling" here, though it's "less hectic" on weekdays.

Eight Mile Creek ◐ Australian
∇ 20 | 13 | 18 | $39

NoLita | 240 Mulberry St. (bet. Prince & Spring Sts.) | 212-431-4635 | www.eightmilecreek.com

Plucky patrons "jump at the chance to try kangaroo" at this NoLita Australian featuring a "well-prepared" sampling of "authentic", low-priced grub; the double-decker "pub" setting also sports a "garden area" and so many "Aussie accents" you'll "swear you're Down Under."

Elephant & Castle ◐ Pub Food
18 | 15 | 18 | $28

G Village | 68 Greenwich Ave. (bet. Perry St. & 7th Ave. S.) | 212-243-1400 | www.elephantandcastle.com

On the Village scene since 1974, this "comforting" joint still "hits the spot" with "enjoyable" pub "basics" and a "hearty brunch", all for dirt-cheap dough; though "snug to the point of claustrophobic", it offers "value" "without pretense" and "you can always get a seat."

El Malecon ◐ Dominican
21 | 9 | 14 | $18

Washington Heights | 4141 Broadway (175th St.) | 212-927-3812
W 90s | 764 Amsterdam Ave. (bet. 97th & 98th Sts.) | 212-864-5648
Bronx | 5592 Broadway (231st St.) | 718-432-5155

Made for "empty stomachs", this Uptown/Bronx trio puts out "stick-to-your-ribs" servings of "mouthwatering rotisserie chicken" and other Dominican "comfort food" for "can't-be-beat" dough; "drab" decor detracts, so regulars often "opt for takeout."

Empanada Mama ◐ S American
22 | 12 | 16 | $16

W 50s | 763 Ninth Ave. (bet. 51st & 52nd Sts.) | 212-698-9008

For a "quickie treat", this Hell's Kitchen South American purveys "freshly made", "come-to-mama" empanadas for all tastes (dessert varieties included) "without breaking the bank"; the "tiny" "hole-in-the-wall" space fills up fast, so many are glad the goods are "portable."

Empire Diner ◐ Diner
15 | 14 | 14 | $25

Chelsea | 210 10th Ave. (22nd St.) | 212-243-2736 | www.empire-diner.com

Like a "time machine", this moderately priced "Chelsea fixture" slings "competent" diner grub 24/7 to everyone from "gallery-hoppers" to "clubbers" drawn to its 1929 "deco charm" and "great outside seating"; it's particularly "cool" at 3 AM, when its young, highly watchable crowd is especially oblivious to the "aloof servers."

	FOOD	DECOR	SERVICE	COST

Energy Kitchen *Health Food* | 15 | 4 | 12 | $14

Chelsea | 307 W. 17th St. (bet. 8th & 9th Aves.) | 212-645-5200
E 40s | 300 E. 41st St. (2nd Ave.) | 212-687-1200
E 50s | 1089 Second Ave. (bet. 57th & 58th Sts.) | 212-888-9300
Financial District | 71 Nassau St. (bet. Fulton & John Sts.) | 212-577-8989 Ⓢ
W 40s | 417 W. 47th St. (9th Ave.) | 212-333-3500
W Village | 82 Christopher St. (bet. Bleecker St. & 7th Ave. S.) |
212-414-8880
www.energykitchen.com

A "gym bunny's best friend", this "no-guilt fast-food" chain offers an "easy" way to "reenergize" on "healthful" burgers, wraps and other "fairly tasty" grub "without making your wallet lose weight"; but given spartan digs and second-class service, many see the "fitness" of takeout.

Erawan *Thai* | 23 | 20 | 20 | $37

Bayside | 213-41 39th Ave. (Bell Blvd.) | Queens | 718-229-1620
Bayside | 42-31 Bell Blvd. (bet. 42nd & 43rd Aves.) | Queens | 718-428-2112
The "tantalizing Thai" menu ranges from "subtle to spicy" at this Bayside twosome that also features Siamese surf 'n' turf at the "nicer", roomier 39th Avenue outlet; "courteous" staffers and "Manhattan quality for Queens prices" explain the "weekend waits."

Ess-a-Bagel *Deli* | 23 | 6 | 13 | $11

E 50s | 831 Third Ave. (bet. 50th & 51st Sts.) | 212-980-1010
Gramercy | 359 First Ave. (21st St.) | 212-260-2252
www.ess-a-bagel.com

"Fresh", "dense" and topped with "whatever your heart desires", the "life preserver"–size bagels vended at this East Side deli duo are "even better when warm out of the oven"; "curmudgeonly" counter service, "bare-bones" decor and "zoo"-like crowds are all "part of the charm."

etcetera etcetera Ⓜ *Italian* | 21 | 19 | 21 | $47

W 40s | 352 W. 44th St. (bet. 8th & 9th Aves.) | 212-399-4141 |
www.etcrestaurant.com

As a "relaxed alternative" to sibling ViceVersa, this Theater District "price performer" proffers "imaginative", "well-prepared" Italian food and "warm" service in an "upbeat", "urban-modern" setting; it can get quite "noisy", so for quieter dining, "request a table upstairs."

	FOOD	DECOR	SERVICE	COST

Excellent Dumpling House ⊄ *Chinese* — 19 | 4 | 11 | $15

Chinatown | 111 Lafayette St. (bet. Canal & Walker Sts.) | 212-219-0212
"Named right", this Chinatown "stalwart" is known for its "fantastic" dumplings and "super-cheap" Shanghai specialties that "make jury duty a pleasure"; be prepared for a "utilitarian" setup with "packed communal tables", but then again "you're not there for the atmosphere."

Felidia *Italian* — 26 | 22 | 24 | $75

E 50s | 243 E. 58th St. (bet. 2nd & 3rd Aves.) | 212-758-1479 | www.lidiasitaly.com
TV guru Lidia Bastianich "lives up to her reputation" at this "*magnifico*" East Side Italian, an "elegant" but "nonintimidating" "benchmark" for "sumptuous cuisine" paired with an "excellent wine list" in a "lovely townhouse" setting; "first-class", "black-tie" service caps a "memorable" performance that "doesn't come cheap" yet "never fails to impress"; N.B. the $30 prix fixe lunch provides Lidia for less.

Ferrara ◑ *Bakery* — 22 | 16 | 16 | $22

Little Italy | 195 Grand St. (bet. Mott & Mulberry Sts.) | 212-226-6150 | www.ferraracafe.com
"Holy cannoli!", you can "gain weight just by breathing the air" at this circa-1892 Little Italy "icon", a "classic" after-dinner stop for "delectable Italian desserts" and "wonderful" espresso; just bear with the "rushed" service and "full-contact" throngs of "locals, tourists and everyone in between"; it's also called "too commercial."

Fette Sau *BBQ* — 24 | 17 | 14 | $25

Williamsburg | 354 Metropolitan Ave. (bet. Havemeyer & Roebling Sts.) | Brooklyn | 718-963-3404
Proof that "hipsters do eat meat", this "garage"-like Williamsburg BBQ (voted No. 1 in NYC) offers a chance to "pig out" on "mouthwatering" 'cue "purchased by weight" in a "cafeteria-type line"; fans perched on "picnic benches" swilling "local lagers" and "smoky bourbons" consider it a bargain "blast."

Fiorentino's *Italian* — 20 | 14 | 18 | $33

Gravesend | 311 Ave. U (bet. McDonald Ave. & West St.) | Brooklyn | 718-372-1445
"When nonna isn't available", this Gravesend "gathering place" is a "tried-and-true" destination for "copious" portions of "homestyle"

Neapolitan *cucina* at a "great price"; the "deafening" digs are always crowded with regulars, so on weekends "you'll have to wait."

Five Guys *Burgers* | 20 | 7 | 13 | $12 |

G Village | 496 La Guardia Pl. (bet. Bleecker & Houston Sts.) | 212-228-6008 ◐

W 50s | 43 W. 55th St. (bet. 5th & 6th Aves.) | 212-459-9600

W Village | 296 Bleecker St. (7th Ave. S.) | 212-367-9200

Brooklyn Heights | 138 Montague St. (bet. Clinton & Henry Sts.) | Brooklyn | 718-797-9380

Park Slope | 284 Seventh Ave. (bet. 6th & 7th Sts.) | Brooklyn | 718-499-9380

College Point | 132-01 14th Ave. (132nd St.) | Queens | 718-767-6500

www.fiveguys.com

"Super-fresh burgers" accessorized with "tons of toppings" "raise the bar for fast food" at this burgeoning DC-based chain that also offers "swoon"-worthy fries and "free peanuts while you wait"; the ambiance is barely "basic", but "budget" diners are "glad to have them here."

Five Points ◐ *American/Mediterranean* | 22 | 21 | 21 | $49 |

NoHo | 31 Great Jones St. (bet. Bowery & Lafayette St.) | 212-253-5700 | www.fivepointsrestaurant.com

"Popular" with "hipster" locals, this "modern" NoHo Med–New American plies "inspired" seasonal dishes and "spot-on" service in a "pretty room" with a "bubbling brook" running through it; the "noise level" aside, it's a "treat" that scores extra points with its "what-a-scene brunch" and $20 prix fixe lunch.

Fleur de Sel *French* | 25 | 21 | 23 | $99 |

Flatiron | 5 E. 20th St. (bet. B'way & 5th Ave.) | 212-460-9100 | www.fleurdeselnyc.com

"Excellence continues" at Cyril Renaud's "classy" Flatiron French, a "treat" for "discriminating" types with prix fixe–only repasts showcasing "*magnifique*" Breton fare paired with "top-of-the-line" wines; "solicitous service" and a "civilized" milieu help justify the high cost, while the $29 lunch deal pleases the "budget-impaired."

Flor de Mayo ◐ *Chinese/Peruvian* | 20 | 8 | 16 | $22 |

W 80s | 484 Amsterdam Ave. (bet. 83rd & 84th Sts.) | 212-787-3388

W 100s | 2651 Broadway (bet. 100th & 101st Sts.) | 212-663-5520

"Succulent", "perfectly seasoned" rotisserie chicken keeps locals flocking to these "dependable" UWS "fallbacks" for "cheap" Chinese-

Peruvian eats; "hectic" vibes, "rushed" service and "diner" decor make a strong case for takeout.

Frank ◐⊅ *Italian* 　　　　　23 | 14 | 16 | $33

E Village | 88 Second Ave. (bet. 5th & 6th Sts.) | 212-420-0202 | www.frankrestaurant.com

"Size doesn't matter" at this ultra-"tiny", no-reservations East Villager offering "simply amazing" "homestyle" Italian food served in "scruffy", "bustling" quarters with "rock-concert" noise levels; considering that the cash-only costs are such a "steal", "long waits" are "inevitable."

Franny's *Pizza* 　　　　　25 | 17 | 20 | $40

Prospect Heights | 295 Flatbush Ave. (bet. Prospect Pl. & St. Marks Ave.) | Brooklyn | 718-230-0221 | www.frannysbrooklyn.com

"Not your ordinary pizza place", this "charming" Prospect Heights venue employs "seasonal" ingredients to create "brilliant" thin-crust pies backed up by "fab pastas" and "amazing cocktails"; no surprise, it draws "killer crowds."

Friedman's Delicatessen *Deli* 　　▽ 21 | 10 | 16 | $23

Chelsea | Chelsea Mkt. | 75 Ninth Ave. (bet. 15th & 16th Sts.) | 212-929-7100 | www.friedmansdeli.com

Chelsea Market's new kosher deli "fills a long-standing need" in the area, serving "serious" Jewish staples including sandwiches piled high with "quality" meats; while the setting's "authentic" enough, it's somehow "not a relaxing place."

Fuleen Seafood ◐ *Chinese/Seafood* 　　23 | 8 | 15 | $29

Chinatown | 11 Division St. (Bowery) | 212-941-6888

"Slam-dunk" seafood with "bold flavors" even lures landlubbers to this "real-deal" Hong Kong–style fish joint in Chinatown; despite "rec-room" ambiance and "bring-an-interpreter" service, the payoffs are a "great bang for your buck" and late-night hours (till 3 AM).

Gahm Mi Oak ◐ *Korean* 　　　　20 | 12 | 13 | $25

Garment District | 43 W. 32nd St. (bet. B'way & 5th Ave.) | 212-695-4113

"Late-night cravings" are answered at this 24/7 Garment District Seoul-fooder best known for its "tasty" *sollongtang* beef soup that some say is "Korean for 'hangover cure'"; "bare-bones" decor and "surly service" to the contrary, it's "fast", "simple" and "always a bargain."

	FOOD	DECOR	SERVICE	COST

Garden Cafe 🔄Ⓜ️ *American* | 28 | 21 | 26 | $54 |

Prospect Heights | 620 Vanderbilt Ave. (Prospect Pl.) | Brooklyn | 718-857-8863

"Like being invited to someone's house for dinner" – "except that someone is a gourmet chef" – this "tiny" Prospect Heights "treasure" is a "charming, intimate" enterprise thanks to the efforts of owners John and Camille Policastro; look for "spectacular" New American food, "perfect hospitality" and prices that are low for the quality, especially that $35 prix fixe dinner.

Gascogne *French* | 21 | 19 | 20 | $49 |

Chelsea | 158 Eighth Ave. (bet. 17th & 18th Sts.) | 212-675-6564 | www.gascognenyc.com

"French expats add atmosphere" to this "quaint" Chelsea bistro purveying "authentic" Southwestern Gallic food and "hospitable" service for fairly "affordable" fares; while the decor's debatable (either "cozy" or "cramped"), there's agreement that the "back garden is perfect" for a "romantic" meal *à deux*.

Gavroche *French* | 17 | 15 | 19 | $44 |

W Village | 212 W. 14th St. (bet. 7th & 8th Aves.) | 212-647-8553 | www.gavroche-ny.com

"Comfortable" and "moderately priced", this "homey" West Village bistro presents "better-than-average" French comfort food in a room that "needs some updating"; still, the "alfresco dining" on its "peaceful" patio "more than makes up for" any shortcomings.

Golden Unicorn *Chinese* | 20 | 12 | 13 | $25 |

Chinatown | 18 E. Broadway, 2nd fl. (Catherine St.) | 212-941-0911 | www.goldenunicornrestaurant.com

It's "dim sum madness" at this "huge" Chinatown "grande dame" where customers "point at items" on the "carts speeding by", or just "eat and guess"; the "bargain" pricing makes the "rude service" and "long lines" more tolerable, though it's "less crazy" if you "go early."

goodburger *Burgers* | 18 | 9 | 13 | $14 |

E 40s | 800 Second Ave. (42nd St.) | 212-922-1700
E 50s | 636 Lexington Ave. (54th St.) | 212-838-6000
Flatiron | 870 Broadway (bet. 17th & 18th Sts.) | 212-529-9100

(continued)

(continued)

goodburger

W 40s | 23 W. 45th St. (bet. 5th & 6th Aves.) | 212-354-0900
www.goodburgerny.com

The "old-fashioned", "made from scratch" burgers at this "extremely casual" mini-chain can be paired with "better-than-good" fries and shakes; too bad the decor and service are barely up to scratch and at times the "loud music prohibits conversation."

Grand Sichuan *Chinese*

22 | 7 | 13 | $24

Chelsea | 229 Ninth Ave. (24th St.) | 212-620-5200 ◐
Chinatown | 125 Canal St. (Chrystie St.) | 212-625-9212 ⇄
E 50s | 1049 Second Ave. (bet. 55th & 56th Sts.) | 212-355-5855
E Village | 19-23 St. Marks Pl. (bet. 2nd & 3rd Aves.) | 212-529-4800
G Village | 15 Seventh Ave. S. (bet. Carmine & Leroy Sts.) | 212-645-0222
Murray Hill | 227 Lexington Ave. (bet. 33rd & 34th Sts.) |
212-679-9770
Rego Park | 98-108 Queens Blvd. (bet. 66th Rd. & 67th Ave.) | Queens |
718-268-8833
www.thegrandsichuan.com

"Richly flavored" Sichuan dishes so "unapologetically spicy" you'll be "sweating like you're in an aerobics class" take center stage at this "cheap", "real-McCoy" mini-chain; "worn-out" looks and "service with a smirk" lead some to opt for "delivery."

Gray's Papaya ◐⇄ *Hot Dogs*

21 | 4 | 13 | $6

Garment District | 539 Eighth Ave. (37th St.) | 212-904-1588
G Village | 402 Sixth Ave. (8th St.) | 212-260-3532
W 70s | 2090 Broadway (72nd St.) | 212-799-0243

Not to be missed, these quintessential 24/7 frank phenomena provide "snappy" hot dogs and "delish" tropical drinks to a "truly democratic" NY crowd; its $4.45 "recession special" may be the best deal in town, trumping the "spartan" digs and "brusque", whaddya-want service.

Great NY Noodle Town ◐⇄ *Noodle Shop*

22 | 5 | 11 | $17

Chinatown | 28½ Bowery (Bayard St.) | 212-349-0923

Insiders recommend the "salt-baked anything" at this "reliable" Chinatown seafood "standby" also known for its "wonderful" noodle soups and "laughably cheap" tabs; "tacky" decor, "nonexistent" service and "contortionist" seating are the downsides.

	FOOD	DECOR	SERVICE	COST

Grimaldi's ⊘ *Pizza*

25 | **11** | **14** | **$21**

Dumbo | 19 Old Fulton St. (bet. Front & Water Sts.) | Brooklyn | 718-858-4300

Douglaston | Douglaston Plaza | 242-02 61st Ave. (bet. Douglaston Pkwy. & 244th St.) | Queens | 718-819-2133

www.grimaldis.com

Just "this side of perfection", the "heavenly thin-crusted" pies piled with "high-quality toppings" make for pizza "masterpieces" at this cash-only Dumbo "stronghold"; long lines are part of this "Brooklyn experience", ditto the "rushed service" and "ordinary" decor; N.B. the new Queens location opened post-Survey.

Hale & Hearty Soups *Sandwiches/Soup*

19 | **7** | **12** | **$11**

Chelsea | Chelsea Mkt. | 75 Ninth Ave. (bet. 15th & 16th Sts.) | 212-255-2400

E 40s | 685 Third Ave. (43rd St.) | 212-681-6460 ✉

E 40s | Grand Central | lower level (42nd St. & Vanderbilt Ave.) | 212-983-2845

E 60s | 849 Lexington Ave. (bet. 64th & 65th Sts.) | 212-517-7600

Financial District | 55 Broad St. (Beaver St.) | 212-509-4100 ✉

Garment District | 462 Seventh Ave. (35th St.) | 212-971-0605 ✉

W 40s | Rockefeller Plaza | 30 Rockefeller Plaza (49th St.) | 212-265-2117 ✉

W 40s | 49 W. 42nd St. (bet. 5th & 6th Aves.) | 212-575-9090 ✉

W 50s | 55 W. 56th St. (bet. 5th & 6th Aves.) | 212-245-9200 ✉

Brooklyn Heights | 32 Court St. (Remsen St.) | Brooklyn | 718-596-5600 ✉

www.haleandhearty.com

"Fast, fresh" sandwiches, salads and a "mind-boggling variety" of "satisfying soups" make up the menu of this "true-to-its-name" chain; despite "AWOL" service and "no decor whatsoever", "long lines" persist at lunchtime, especially during "bikini season."

Hampton Chutney Co. *Indian*

19 | **9** | **13** | **$16**

SoHo | 68 Prince St. (bet. Crosby & Lafayette Sts.) | 212-226-9996

W 80s | 464 Amsterdam Ave. (bet. 82nd & 83rd Sts.) | 212-362-5050

www.hamptonchutney.com

Offering "cheap, delicious dosas", these Indian fusion practitioners are highly touted as "healthful" alternatives to fast food; while the

SoHo branch is a hipster scene and the UWS more of a "mommy-and-me" magnet, both provide big "bang for your buck."

Hill Country *BBQ*

21 | 16 | 13 | $33

Chelsea | 30 W. 26th St. (bet. B'way & 6th Ave.) | 212-255-4544 | www.hillcountryny.com

Texas Hill Country lands in Chelsea via this "cavernous" BBQ specialist in a "beat-up honky-tonk" setting where the food is ordered "cafeteria-style", "served on butcher paper" and consumed at long "communal tables"; fans find it "seriously delicious", but foes fret over the "tedious" "serve-yourself" process.

Hummus Place ● *Israeli/Vegetarian*

23 | 9 | 15 | $16

E Village | 109 St. Marks Pl. (bet. Ave. A & 1st Ave.) | 212-529-9198
G Village | 71 Seventh Ave. S. (bet. Barrow & Bleecker Sts.) | 212-924-2022
G Village | 99 MacDougal St. (bet. Bleecker & W. 3rd Sts.) | 212-533-3089
W 70s | 305 Amsterdam Ave. (bet. 74th & 75th Sts.) | 212-799-3335
www.hummusplace.com

"World-class hummus" is "all they have and all they need" at this Israeli quartet where the namesake dish "puts the supermarket version to shame"; despite "crowded", "bare-bones" settings and "oblivious" (albeit "fast") service, the "dirt-cheap prices" make fans "hope they never pita out."

Indus Valley *Indian*

22 | 15 | 19 | $32

W 100s | 2636 Broadway (100th St.) | 212-222-9222 | www.indusvalleyusa.com

"Fragrant, flavorful" Indian food with "just the right amount of heat" turns up at this "elite" Upper Westsider flaunting plenty of "downtown style"; though you'll "spend more than on Sixth Street", the $12.95 prix fixe lunch buffet is a bona fide "bargain."

Ippudo ● *Japanese*

∇ 25 | 23 | 22 | $26

E Village | 65 Fourth Ave. (bet. 9th & 10th Sts.) | 212-388-0088 | www.ippudo.com/ny/

Famed for its "silky" signature tonkotsu ramen, this "real-deal" East Village link of a Japanese chain is the latest contender for the title of "Noodle Heaven"; "inexpensive" costs and a "cool" setting make it a "force to be reckoned with", hence the "long waits."

	FOOD	DECOR	SERVICE	COST

Island Burgers & Shakes *Burgers* — 22 | 8 | 15 | $17

W 50s | 766 Ninth Ave. (bet. 51st & 52nd Sts.) | 212-307-7934 | www.islandburgersny.com

Big "messy burgers" with a "seemingly infinite choice of toppings" washed down with "dreamy shakes" are the hooks at this surf-themed Hell's Kitchen "staple"; "low costs" distract from the "no-frills" decor and the much-lamented "lack of french fries."

I Trulli *Italian* — 23 | 21 | 20 | $58

Gramercy | 122 E. 27th St. (bet. Lexington Ave. & Park Ave. S.) | 212-481-7372 | www.itrulli.com

"Becoming an institution", this 15-year-old Gramercy Italian specializes in "authentic Pugliese" cuisine served in rustically "romantic" environs enhanced by a "cozy" fireplace in winter and a "lovely garden" in summer; a "brilliant wine list" (decanted at the adjoining enoteca) and a $24 set-price lunch help distract from the otherwise "upscale" pricing.

Jackson Diner ⊅ *Indian* — 21 | 10 | 15 | $23

Jackson Heights | 37-47 74th St. (bet. Roosevelt & 37th Aves.) | Queens | 718-672-1232 | www.jacksondiner.com

Fans "savor the flavors" at this "lively" Jackson Heights Indian that's best known for its "exceptional" $9.95 brunch buffet; "patience-testing lines" and "no charm" in the looks department are downsides, but the low prices and fine food "go a long way" to make up for it.

Jaiya Thai *Thai* — 22 | 9 | 15 | $29

Gramercy | 396 Third Ave. (28th St.) | 212-889-1330 | www.jaiya.com

They "really turn up the heat" at this Gramercy Thai where even mild dishes tend toward the "spicier end of the spectrum"; though "bargain" bills blunt below-standard decor and service, many still prefer takeout.

Jean Georges ⓩ *French* — 28 | 26 | 27 | $127

W 60s | Trump Int'l Hotel | 1 Central Park W. (bet. 60th & 61st Sts.) | 212-299-3900 | www.jean-georges.com

A "class act from start to finish", Jean-Georges Vongerichten's Columbus Circle flagship "continues to dazzle" with "top-rung", "ever-evolving" New French prix fixes that "simultaneously comfort and excite", served by a "read-your-mind" staff in a beautifully "understated", "modern" setting; jackets are required for this "practically perfect" dining experience, and though prices are "not for the weak of pocket-

	FOOD	DECOR	SERVICE	COST

book", most agree it's "worth every cent" and say the $24 set-price lunch (in the "more casual" Nougatine Room) is the "best deal in town", rivaled only by the main room's $28 lunch "steal."

Jewel of India *Indian*

19	17	19	$39

W 40s | 15 W. 44th St. (bet. 5th & 6th Aves.) | 212-869-5544 | www.jewelofindiarestaurant.com

"Affordable", "above-average" Indian standards, "attentive" service and a "comfortable" setting have made this bi-level Midtowner a "reliable" stop for 20 years; insiders say downstairs is "better" than upstairs and the $16.95 "lunch buffet deal" is most "satisfying" of all.

J.G. Melon ◐⊅ *Pub Food*

21	12	15	$26

E 70s | 1291 Third Ave. (74th St.) | 212-744-0585

The burgers and cottage fries blow away the rest of the "buttoned-down comfort-food" menu offered at this longtime UES pub; despite "cranky" staffers and a "cash-only" rule, it's a "preppy" magnet thanks to its "college-days"-meets-"country-club" aura.

Jing Fong *Chinese*

19	12	11	$21

Chinatown | 20 Elizabeth St. (bet. Bayard & Canal Sts.) | 212-964-5256

You can "feel the floor vibrating" at this "mammoth" Chinatown "dim sum circus" offering a "massive variety" of "tasty" Hong Kong–style treats; "dirt-cheap" tabs, "deafening" decibels and "no-English" service are all part of the "chaotic", "Vegas"-esque package.

Joe Allen ◐ *American*

17	16	18	$42

W 40s | 326 W. 46th St. (bet. 8th & 9th Aves.) | 212-581-6464 | www.joeallenrestaurant.com

A "theatrical institution", this West 40s American dishes "reliable" comfort chow to show-goers and "drunk actors" alike; sure, the decor's "stale" and service depends on whether "your waiter had a good audition that day", but it's a "safe bet" for "casual" grazing at a "modest" cost.

Joe & Pat's *Italian/Pizza*

22	11	18	$21

Staten Island | 1758 Victory Blvd. (Manor Rd.) | 718-981-0887 | www.joeandpatsny.com

"Delicious" pies with "paper-thin crusts" make for "pizza perfection" at this circa-1960 Staten Island "favorite"; despite dinerlike decor and "loud" acoustics, it's a bargain neighborhood "staple."

	FOOD	DECOR	SERVICE	COST

Joe's Pizza *Pizza*

23	5	13	$9

G Village | 7 Carmine St. (bet. Bleecker St. & 6th Ave.) | 212-255-3946 ●
Midwood | 1621 Kings Hwy. (E. 16th St.) | Brooklyn | 718-339-4525 ⊟
Park Slope | 137 Seventh Ave. (bet. Carroll St. & Garfield Pl.) | Brooklyn |
718-398-9198

These separately owned pizzerias produce "chewy", "fresh-from-the-oven" pies made with "artful crusts" and "fresh mozzarella"; given the "divey", "hole-in-the-wall" setups, takeout is recommended – just "try not to lick the delivery box."

Joe's Shanghai *Chinese*

22	9	14	$24

Chinatown | 9 Pell St. (bet. Bowery & Mott St.) | 212-233-8888 ⊟
W 50s | 24 W. 56th St. (bet. 5th & 6th Aves.) | 212-333-3868
Flushing | 136-21 37th Ave. (bet. Main & Union Sts.) | Queens |
718-539-3838 ⊟
www.joeshanghairestaurants.com

"Unbeatable soup dumplings" are the "highlight" of this Shanghainese trio that's usually "crowded with tourists and Zagat readers"; "greasy-spoon" decor, "long lines" and "shared tables" come with the territory, but all is forgiven after one bite of its "cheap", "tasty" morsels.

John's Pizzeria *Pizza*

22	13	15	$23

E 60s | 408 E. 64th St. (bet. 1st & York Aves.) | 212-935-2895
G Village | 278 Bleecker St. (bet. 6th Ave. & 7th Ave. S.) |
212-243-1680 ●⊟
W 40s | 260 W. 44th St. (bet. B'way & 8th Ave.) | 212-391-7560 ●
www.johnspizzerianyc.com

"Long lines" prove that this "classic" pizzeria trio "deserves its rep" as the "granddaddy" of "crispy, brick-oven perfection" – even if "molasses"-slow service and a "no-slices" policy detract; though purists plainly prefer the 80-year-old Village original, Midtown's "converted church" setting is "perfect" pre-theater.

Joya ⊟ *Thai*

23	17	18	$22

Cobble Hill | 215 Court St. (bet. Warren & Wyckoff Sts.) | Brooklyn |
718-222-3484

"Better-than-Bangkok" Thai food at "bargain" tabs keeps this "hip", cash-only Cobble Hiller "always mobbed"; "strong" drinks, "quick" service and a "sexy industrial" setting fuel the "vibrant buzz", but if "blaring" dance music ain't your thing, "try for a table in the garden."

	FOOD	DECOR	SERVICE	COST

Junior's *Diner*
17 | 11 | 15 | $26

E 40s | Grand Central | lower level (42nd St. & Vanderbilt Ave.) | 212-983-5257
W 40s | Shubert Alley | 1515 Broadway (enter on 45th St., bet. B'way & 8th Ave.) | 212-302-2000 ●
Downtown Bklyn | 386 Flatbush Ave. Ext. (DeKalb Ave.) | Brooklyn | 718-852-5257 ●
www.juniorscheesecake.com
"Sublime cheesecake" is all you need to know about this Downtown Brooklyn "classic" dispensing "giant" portions of "the usual" deli offerings in "schmaltzy" digs; the less atmospheric Manhattan branches are "convenient" if catching a show or train.

Kampuchea Ⓜ *Cambodian*
▽ 21 | 17 | 17 | $31

LES | 78 Rivington St. (Allen St.) | 212-529-3901 | www.kampucheanyc.com
"Flavorful" noodles, sandwiches and other Khmer street food make up the menu of this Lower East Side Cambodian "find"; the "uncomfortable seating" and "loud" acoustics are tempered by "relaxed" service and "inexpensive" tabs.

Kang Suh ● *Korean*
21 | 11 | 15 | $35

Garment District | 1250 Broadway (32nd St.) | 212-564-6845
"Tasty at all hours", this 24/7 Garment District Korean offers "sizzling", do-it-yourself BBQ as well as a host of other "reliable" menu options (including sushi) at low cost; it's been a "Manhattan fixture" for 25 years, despite "no atmosphere" and "rushed service."

Kati Roll Co. *Indian*
22 | 6 | 12 | $11

Garment District | 49 W. 39th St. (bet. 5th & 6th Aves.) | 212-730-4280
G Village | 99 MacDougal St. (bet. Bleecker & W. 3rd Sts.) | 212-420-6517 ●
www.thekatirollcompany.com
"Late-night" revelers seeking "cheap snacks" tout the "fantastic" namesake rolls (aka Indian burritos) at these Midtown/Village storefronts; "long lines", "slow" service and sari decor to the contrary, fans "keep coming back."

Katz's Delicatessen *Deli*
23 | 9 | 12 | $22

LES | 205 E. Houston St. (Ludlow St.) | 212-254-2246 | www.katzdeli.com
"Loud and crowded, just like NY", this "frozen-in-time" LES deli "where Harry met Sally" ("I'll have what she's having") is famous for its "un-

	FOOD	DECOR	SERVICE	COST

surpassed" pastrami, service "with a snarl" and total "lack of decor" –
unless you consider Formica decor; although it can be tough to "find a
seat" or get the counterman's attention, it's a slice of "cultural history"
that everyone should experience.

Kings' Carriage House *American*

21	25	23	$72

E 80s | 251 E. 82nd St. (bet. 2nd & 3rd Aves.) | 212-734-5490 |
www.kingscarriagehouse.com

An "elegant townhouse location" lends this "adult" UES New American
a "hideaway" feel, while ultra-"charming" decor, "delicious" prix fixe
menus and "gracious service" make it "perfect for celebrations or romance"; sure, it's "expensive", so "value"-seekers show up for high tea
or the bargain $18.95 lunch special.

Kittichai *Thai*

22	27	20	$60

SoHo | 60 Thompson Hotel | 60 Thompson St. (bet. Broome & Spring Sts.) |
212-219-2000 | www.kittichairestaurant.com

"Theatrical" decor (including a "pond with floating candles and or-
chids") nearly overwhelms the "innovative" food at this "so-hip-it-
hurts" Thai where "stylish" sorts struggle to be heard over the "loud
music"; sure, "it's pricey" – unless you opt for the bargain $30 pre-
theater menu – and the "modellike" staff exudes "attitude", but let's
face it, "it's SoHo."

Kuma Inn Ⓜ📵 *Filipino/Thai*

24	13	19	$35

LES | 113 Ludlow St., 2nd fl. (bet. Delancey & Rivington Sts.) | 212-353-8866 |
www.kumainn.com

"Don't be put off by the stairwell entrance" of this second-floor LES
"hideaway" – it's "worth seeking out" for its "refined" Filipino-Thai
small-plate fare; the "friendly" vibe, "reasonable" prices and BYO policy make up for the tiny, no-frills digs.

Kum Gang San ❶ *Korean*

21	15	16	$33

Garment District | 49 W. 32nd St. (bet. B'way & 5th Ave.) | 212-967-0909
Flushing | 138-28 Northern Blvd. (bet. Bowne & Union Sts.) | Queens |
718-461-0909
www.kumgangsan.net

These "bustling" 24-hour Koreans offer "tasty" BBQ and other classics; "fast-paced" service means meals may not be leisurely, but they're
"lots of fun" thanks to "kitschy" decor elements.

	FOOD	DECOR	SERVICE	COST

La Bergamote *Bakery/French* `24` `13` `15` `$14`
Chelsea | 169 Ninth Ave. (20th St.) | 212-627-9010
W 50s | 515 W. 52nd St. (bet. 10th & 11th Aves.) | 212-586-2429
A "treat every time", this Chelsea bakery/cafe's "splendidly tempting" pastries and other Gallic goods are "exquisite to the eye, palate" and pocketbook; "cramped" digs don't deter the faithful, ditto the "politely indifferent" service; N.B. the 52nd Street offshoot opened post-Survey.

La Flor Bakery & Cafe ⊅ *Bakery* `24` `15` `18` `$24`
Woodside | 53-02 Roosevelt Ave. (53rd St.) | Queens | 718-426-8023
The Mexican chef-owner "brings his homeland to life" through an eclectic mix of "scrumptious" savories and sweets at this cheap, cash-only bakery/cafe tucked under the 7 el in Woodside; expect a wait since it's "too small" and service can be "flaky."

La Lanterna di Vittorio ☽ *Italian* `19` `22` `17` `$27`
G Village | 129 MacDougal St. (bet. W. 3rd & 4th Sts.) | 212-529-5945 | www.lalanternacaffe.com
You feel you've been "whisked away from the hustle and bustle" at this "cozy" Village Italian supplying "quality" pizzas, pastas and desserts that don't "break the bank"; "working fireplaces", a "tranquil" en-closed garden and "cool" live jazz add up to the "perfect date place."

La Méditerranée *French* `19` `16` `19` `$48`
E 50s | 947 Second Ave. (bet. 50th & 51st Sts.) | 212-755-4155 | www.lamediterraneeny.com
A "throwback to the way French restaurants used to be", this Midtown Provençal is an "unassuming", "affordable" choice for "solid" cooking delivered by a "welcoming" crew; a pianist's "tuneful music" ups the "romance" quotient (Thursday–Saturday nights).

Land *Thai* `22` `17` `18` `$27`
E 80s | 1565 Second Ave. (bet. 81st & 82nd Sts.) | 212-439-1847
W 80s | 450 Amsterdam Ave. (bet. 81st & 82nd Sts.) | 212-501-8121
www.landthaikitchen.com
You can "expect a wait" at this Crosstown Thai twosome, but "it's worth it" according to admirers who "squeeze in like sardines" for "creative", "spicy" dishes that "make you sweat with joy"; "speedy" service and "cool", "mod" digs are enticements, but it's "bargain prices" that seal the deal.

	FOOD	DECOR	SERVICE	COST

L & B Spumoni Gardens *Dessert/Pizza* | 23 | 10 | 15 | $22 |

Bensonhurst | 2725 86th St. (bet. 10th & 11th Sts.) | Brooklyn | 718-449-6921 | www.spumonigardens.com

The "ethereally light" Sicilian squares and "creamy" spumoni inspire hyperbole ("the best ever!") at this Bensonhurst "staple" that has a certain *"Saturday Night Fever"* vibe though it opened when FDR was in office; "get here early" 'cause "tables inside and out fill up fast."

Landmark Tavern *American/Irish* | 17 | 18 | 18 | $36 |

W 40s | 626 11th Ave. (46th St.) | 212-247-2562 | www.thelandmarktavern.org

A "vestige of time gone by", this circa-1868 Hell's Kitchen tavern offers moderately priced Irish-American pub fare that's "only slightly more updated" than the "old NY" digs (and that's a good thing); it's worth a visit for the "history" alone, but it's also an "atmospheric" party venue whose scotch list that "goes on for miles" provides another reason to trek west.

La Petite Auberge *French* | 19 | 15 | 21 | $47 |

Gramercy | 116 Lexington Ave. (bet. 27th & 28th Sts.) | 212-689-5003 | www.lapetiteaubergeny.com

Meant to evoke an eatery in one of "Brittany's villages", this "quaint" "fixed-in-time" Gramercy French keeps cranking out "reliably appealing" bistro classics as well as a can't-be-beat $28 dinner prix fixe; sure, "it could use sprucing up", but "who cares?" – it's mercifully "without the attitude" of its "too-cool" competitors.

La Pizza Fresca Ristorante *Italian* | 22 | 16 | 17 | $39 |

Flatiron | 31 E. 20th St. (bet. B'way & Park Ave. S.) | 212-598-0141 | www.lapizzafrescaristorante.com

A "fantastic little find", this Flatiron Italian proffers "surprisingly good" brick-oven pizzas and other "straight-off-the-boat" staples, but it's best known for its "impressive" wines; "service can be a bit slow", but at least the staff's "friendly."

La Taza de Oro ☒⇥ *Diner* | 18 | 6 | 17 | $16 |

Chelsea | 96 Eighth Ave. (bet. 14th & 15th Sts.) | 212-243-9946

Definitely "it's a dive", but this coffee shop is a "true Chelsea original" dishing up "cheap", "satisfying", "down-home" Puerto Rican eats in "easy" environs; a "charming survivor" in an evolving area, this bar-

| | FOOD | DECOR | SERVICE | COST |

gain "slice of old New York" "has been around" for 50-plus years for lots of good reasons.

Le Cirque ☑ French
24 | 25 | 24 | $120

E 50s | One Beacon Court | 151 E. 58th St. (bet. Lexington & 3rd Aves.) | 212-644-0202 | www.lecirque.com

"There's always a show" at "consummate ringmaster" Sirio Maccioni's "fabled" Midtowner, where the "refined" French cuisine and "impeccable" service are the "epitome of NY swank", bested only by "stunning" "big-top" decor and a caravan of "vintage rich-and-famous" faces; just remember to "dress up" (jackets required) and prepare to "pay dearly", though for "less expensive" tabs "without pomp", try the new adjacent wine-and-tapas lounge that's run by Sirio's talented sons.

Lenny's *Sandwiches*
18 | 7 | 14 | $14

E 50s | 1024 Second Ave. (54th St.) | 212-355-5700
E 60s | 1269 First Ave. (68th St.) | 212-288-0852
E 70s | 1481 Second Ave. (77th St.) | 212-288-5288
Financial District | 108 John St. (bet. Cliff & Pearl Sts.) | 212-385-2828
Flatiron | 16 W. 23rd St. (5th Ave.) | 212-462-4433
G Village | 418 Sixth Ave. (9th St.) | 212-353-0300
W 40s | 60 W. 48th St. (bet. 5th & 6th Aves.) | 212-997-1969
W 40s | 613 Ninth Ave. (43rd St.) | 212-957-7800
W 70s | 302 Columbus Ave. (74th St.) | 212-580-8300
W 80s | 489 Columbus Ave. (84th St.) | 212-787-9368
www.lennysnyc.com

"Fresh" "deli-style" sandwiches with "countless toppings" for not a lot of bread – "what's not to like?" muse groupies of this "lunchtime staple" chain; its "bare-bones" setups can be "uninviting", but "road-runner" service means you won't linger long.

Leo's Latticini ☑ *Deli/Italian*
▽ 25 | 12 | 21 | $14
(aka Mama's of Corona)

Corona | 46-02 104th St. (46th Ave.) | Queens | 718-898-6069

This third-generation "family-run" Italian deli remains a "wonderful" Corona landmark for "unbelievable" heros featuring the "best" "housemade mozz"; incredibly "cheap" prices for mega-meals and famously "friendly" service are other "high points" – as for decor, delis aren't supposed to have much.

	FOOD	DECOR	SERVICE	COST

Le Pain Quotidien *Bakery/Belgian* | 18 | 15 | 13 | $23 |

E 60s | 833 Lexington Ave. (bet. 63rd & 64th Sts.) | 212-755-5810
E 70s | 252 E. 77th St. (bet. 2nd & 3rd Aves.) | 212-249-8600
E 80s | 1131 Madison Ave. (bet. 84th & 85th Sts.) | 212-327-4900
Flatiron | ABC Carpet & Home | 38 E. 19th St. (bet. B'way & Park Ave. S.) | 212-673-7900
G Village | 10 Fifth Ave. (8th St.) | 212-253-2324
G Village | 801 Broadway (11th St.) | 212-677-5277
SoHo | 100 Grand St. (bet. Greene & Mercer Sts.) | 212-625-9009
W 50s | 922 Seventh Ave. (58th St.) | 212-757-0775
W 60s | 60 W. 65th St. (bet. B'way & CPW) | 212-721-4001
W 70s | 50 W. 72nd St. (bet. Columbus Ave. & CPW) | 212-712-9700
www.painquotidien.com

"*Fantastique*" "European-style" breads, sandwiches and other "wholesome", "largely organic" "light bites" keep this Belgian bakery/cafe chain "bustling and noisy"; the "rustic" interiors outfitted with "wooden communal tables" and "slow", "spacey" service rate a bit less well.

Le Refuge *French* | 20 | 19 | 20 | $58 |

E 80s | 166 E. 82nd St. (bet. Lexington & 3rd Aves.) | 212-861-4505 | www.lerefugenyc.com

"You don't have to cross the pond" to "feel like you're in France" thanks to this "time-tested" UES bistro serving "delicious" "provincial" French fare in a "relaxed" "country-house" setting, complete with "pleasant" garden; "charming" service enhances the "old-world" feel, but prices are strictly "up to date" – save for the $32 prix fixe dinner.

Le Singe Vert ● *French* | 18 | 16 | 16 | $41 |

Chelsea | 160 Seventh Ave. (bet. 19th & 20th Sts.) | 212-366-4100 | www.lesingevert.com

"Close your eyes" and "you're on the Left Bank" at this "*très* French" Chelsea bistro dispensing "decent" classics with "authentic" flair; "crowded" quarters are "part of the experience", but you can "escape" to sidewalk tables in warm weather and enjoy its $29 pre-theater dinner.

Lombardi's 孕 *Pizza* | 24 | 12 | 15 | $23 |

NoLita | 32 Spring St. (bet. Mott & Mulberry Sts.) | 212-941-7994 | www.firstpizza.com

For a "slice of pizza history", head to this NoLita "landmark" whose "classic" coal-fired pies are beloved for their "perfectly thin", "crispy, slightly

| | FOOD | DECOR | SERVICE | COST |

charred" crusts and "fresh, authentic" toppings; however, its perpetual-"favorite" status spells "absurd waits" and "noisy", "cramped" quarters.

Lucali ₱ *Pizza* | 27 | 19 | 19 | $21

Carroll Gardens | 575 Henry St. (bet. Carroll St. & 1st Pl.) | Brooklyn | 718-858-4086

This Carroll Gardens upstart is voted this year's No. 1 for pizza in NYC thanks to its "sublime", "perfectly thin-crusted" pies and calzones turned out by "brick-oven" maestro/owner Mark Iacono; its "small" space has an "old-world" feel and lots of "local flavor", but "there's always a wait" so "call ahead to get your name on the list."

Mama's Food Shop ⊠₱ *American* | 21 | 9 | 13 | $16

E Village | 200 E. Third St. (bet. Aves. A & B) | 212-777-4425 | www.mamasfoodshop.com

For "heaping portions" of "tasty comfort food" – including "heavenly mac 'n' cheese" – head to this East Village American that's among the "best bargains in town"; those who think the "cafeteria-type" setup and attitudinous "hipster" service "could be better" opt for takeout.

Mancora ● *Peruvian* | ∇ 22 | 14 | 21 | $28

E Village | 99 First Ave. (6th St.) | 212-253-1011

At this "homey" East Village Peruvian, the "delicious", "value"-oriented specialties ("huge, fresh platters of ceviche", the "best chicken I've had in ages") are "presented with pride"; the decor may be "modest", but it "never fails to welcome."

Mandarin Court *Chinese* | 21 | 9 | 13 | $22

Chinatown | 61 Mott St. (bet. Bayard & Canal Sts.) | 212-608-3838

"Cheap, tasty, plentiful – who could ask for more?" muse admirers of this "no-frills" Chinatown dim sum dowager; it's best to "ignore the surly staff, Formica tables" and "weekend crowds" and just focus on those "heavenly" cart-borne tidbits.

Mandoo Bar *Korean* | 20 | 11 | 17 | $20

Garment District | 2 W. 32nd St. (bet. B'way & 5th Ave.) | 212-279-3075

Look for the "cooks making fresh dumplings at the window" and you've found this "tiny", "simple" Garment District Korean known for its namesake bundles "so good you could cry"; it's just the thing for a "quick, cheap" bite, even if purists question its authenticity.

	FOOD	DECOR	SERVICE	COST

Maria Pia *Italian*   19 | 16 | 18 | $39

W 50s | 319 W. 51st St. (bet. 8th & 9th Aves.) | 212-765-6463 |
www.mariapianyc.com

"Reliable" "before a Broadway show" when its $22 dinner special is in
full swing, this Theater District Italian offers "above-average" fare at
solid "value" in a neighborhood short on bargains; with digs on the
"small side", it gets "crowded" and "noisy" during pre-curtain hours,
so try for the "treasure" of a back garden.

Marseille ● *French/Mediterranean*   20 | 18 | 19 | $47

W 40s | 630 Ninth Ave. (44th St.) | 212-333-3410 |
www.marseillenyc.com

For "sophisticated" dining in Hell's Kitchen, try this "informal" yet
"civilized" French-Med offering "terrific" eats and an "authentic brasserie" setup complete with "wonderful bar"; it's "fabulous pre-theater"
thanks to a $35 prix fixe and a "pleasant" staff that "gets you in and
out" without making you feel "herded."

Matsugen *Japanese*   ∇ 21 | 19 | 21 | $77

TriBeCa | 241 Church St. (Leonard St.) | 212-925-0202 |
www.jean-georges.com

A Japanese soba house gone "upscale", Jean-Georges Vongerichten's
TriBeCa newcomer plies "made-on-site" buckwheat noodles in every
iteration, plus other "refined" "classics" such as shabu-shabu and
sushi, in the sleek "understated" space that formerly housed 66; early
reports call it "promising", and the price is right as long as you stick
to the noodles.

McCormick & Schmick's *Seafood*   20 | 18 | 19 | $53

W 50s | 1285 Sixth Ave. (enter on 52nd St., bet. 6th & 7th Aves.) |
212-459-1222 | www.mccormickandschmicks.com

Yes, it's a "chain", but this Midtown seafooder "swims to the top" of
the genre with its "reliable" catch served in "bustling" digs perfect for
"business lunch"; snobs say it would fit better in a "suburban mall" –
but then it wouldn't be so "convenient" "pre-Radio City"; its $30 pre-
theater special is a steal.

Megu *Japanese*   24 | 26 | 23 | $87

TriBeCa | 62 Thomas St. (bet. Church St. & W. B'way) | 212-964-7777
(continued)

(continued)

Megu Midtown ⚅ *Japanese*

E 40s | Trump World Tower | 845 United Nations Plaza (1st Ave. & 47th St.) | 212-964-7777
www.megunyc.com

As "memorable dining experiences" go, it's hard to top this "theatrical" Japanese twosome whose "luxurious" cuisine and "thoughtful" service are outdone only by the "beautiful", "over-the-top" decor centered around a "giant Buddha" ice sculpture; the Midtown branch exudes more of a "business vibe", with "pretty people" gravitating to the TriBeCa original where a good-deal prix fixe lunch is only $25.

Métisse *French*

19 | 16 | 19 | $43

W 100s | 239 W. 105th St. (bet. Amsterdam Ave. & B'way) | 212-666-8825 | www.metisserestaurant.com

"One of the best" in the restaurant-challenged neighborhood "near Columbia", this "charming" French bistro keeps 'em coming back with its "reliable", "reasonably priced" classics and "warm" service; its "comfortable" setting is "nothing fancy", but that suits the locals just fine.

Metrazur ⚅ *American*

20 | 21 | 18 | $53

E 40s | Grand Central | East Balcony (42nd St. & Vanderbilt Ave.) | 212-687-4600 | www.charliepalmer.com

"Worth missing your train for", Charlie Palmer's "so New York City" New American in Grand Central Terminal is a "magical place" thanks to its "balcony" seating "overlooking the Concourse"; maybe the overall experience is "expensive" "for what you get", but the "people-watching" is beyond compare and they do offer a $35 prix fixe dinner.

Mia Dona *Italian*

21 | 18 | 19 | $53

E 50s | 206 E. 58th St. (bet. 2nd & 3rd Aves.) | 212-750-8170 | www.miadona.com

Michael Psilakis and Donatella Arpaia "have created another winner" with this "welcoming" East Side Italian featuring "rustic" yet "innovative" fare in "sleek" (some say "sterile") environs; though the staff perhaps is "still getting its footing", most agree that overall it's "off to a good start" and the $25 lunch is a steal.

	FOOD	DECOR	SERVICE	COST

Mill Basin Kosher Deli *Deli*
| 22 | 15 | 17 | $25 |

Mill Basin | 5823 Ave. T (59th St.) | Brooklyn | 718-241-4910 |
www.millbasindeli.com

"Humongous sandwiches" are the signature of this "quality kosher deli" in Mill Basin, a "throwback" destination for "delish" "Jewish specialties" that does double-duty as a "fine art" gallery with "Ertés and Lichtensteins" on display.

Mill Korean *Korean*
| 18 | 13 | 15 | $22 |

W 100s | 2895 Broadway (bet. 112th & 113th Sts.) | 212-666-7653

"Students and locals" "don't have to go all the way Downtown" for a "solid" Korean "fix" thanks to this UWS "stalwart"; service is "abrupt" and the "small" setup's "not all that comfortable", but great "value" keeps it "active."

Milos, Estiatorio ● *Greek/Seafood*
| 27 | 23 | 23 | $79 |

W 50s | 125 W. 55th St. (bet. 6th & 7th Aves.) | 212-245-7400 |
www.milos.ca

It's like "landing in Athens" "without jet lag" at this "top-of-the-line" Midtown Greek, a "superior" source for "fabulously prepared", "fresher-than-fresh" seafood served with "panache" in a "grand", "airy" space; just prepare for pricing "as if Onassis were at your table", especially if you're "paying by the pound"; though, for a less-expensive option, go for the $24 prix fixe lunch.

Minca ●⊅ *Japanese*
| ▽ 22 | 11 | 17 | $18 |

E Village | 536 E. Fifth St. (bet. Aves. A & B) | 212-505-8001

Ramen mavens "greedily slurp up" a "lip-smacking" variety of "hearty" noodle soups at this "tiny" East Villager, a "quick", cost-effective choice for "authentic" Japanese "comfort food"; its "neighborhood secret" status means "nabbing a seat" is easier here than at many competitors in the area.

Moim Ⓜ *Korean*
| 24 | 23 | 19 | $41 |

Park Slope | 206 Garfield Pl. (bet. 7th & 8th Aves.) | Brooklyn | 718-499-8092 |
www.moimrestaurant.com

"Super" "modern spins on classic dishes" earn "raves" for this "stylish" Park Slope Korean, a neighborhood "knockout" for "innovative" eating at a fair price; the "noise level escalates" as "yuppified" fans fill its "chic space", though a garden "oasis" is in the works.

	FOOD	DECOR	SERVICE	COST

Momofuku Noodle Bar *Noodle Shop*   `23` `14` `17` `$31`
E Village | 171 First Ave. (bet. 10th & 11th Sts.) | 212-777-7773 |
www.momofuku.com
"The hype is justified" at David Chang's "stark", "eternally packed"
East Villager, a "casual" communal showcase for Japanese-accented
New American fare centered on "ethereal" noodle soups and "transcendent" pork buns; it now occupies "expanded" quarters, but it's
still "tight", "rushed" and well "worth the hassle."

Momofuku Ssäm Bar 🛇 *American*   `23` `15` `17` `$41`
E Village | 207 Second Ave. (13th St.) | 212-254-3500 | www.momofuku.com
Admiring multitudes "can't get enough" of David Chang's "brilliant"
"flavor combos" at this roomier East Village adjunct of his Noodle Bar,
an "informal" destination for "luscious" Asian-influenced New
American creations; whether for burrito-esque *ssäms* at lunch or a
"more sophisticated" dinner, the "bench seating" "fills up fast" so "be
prepared to wait."

Nam *Vietnamese*   `21` `17` `19` `$39`
TriBeCa | 110 Reade St. (W. B'way) | 212-267-1777 | www.namnyc.com
A "trendy crowd" veers "off the beaten path" to this "hip" TriBeCan to
"mix it up" with "excellent", "adventurous" Vietnamese eats in a
"lively" setting; overseen by an "efficient" team, it's "worth the trek"
for its "appealing" ambiance and "good value."

New Bo-Ky ⊅ *Noodle Shop*   `▽ 20` `4` `9` `$12`
Chinatown | 80 Bayard St. (bet. Mott & Mulberry Sts.) |
212-406-2292
It's "worth being on jury duty" for a chance to sample the "wide selection" of "out-of-this-world" Chinese and Vietnamese noodle soups at
this "real-deal" C-town "staple"; the surroundings and service are "ab-
solutely bare-bones", but you "really can't beat" the cost.

Nha Trang *Vietnamese*   `21` `7` `15` `$17`
Chinatown | 148 Centre St. (bet. Walker & White Sts.) | 212-941-9292
Chinatown | 87 Baxter St. (bet. Bayard & Canal Sts.) | 212-233-5948
This "hole-in-the-wall" Chinatown twosome is "well-vetted" for "plentiful" portions of "awesome" "Vietnamese favorites" served in the
"blink of an eye" at "low, low prices"; sure, they're seriously "plain",
but devotees "don't go for the decor."

	FOOD	DECOR	SERVICE	COST

Nice Green Bo 🍽 *Chinese*   23 | 5 | 11 | $18
(fka New Green Bo)

Chinatown | 66 Bayard St. (bet. Elizabeth & Mott Sts.) | 212-625-2359
"Juicy soup dumplings" "are the stars" at this "popular" Chinatowner,
where the "super" Shanghainese chow comes "practically free"; the
new name's a little nicer, but the "dingy" digs, "jammed" "communal
seating" and "in-and-out" service are anything but.

Nicky's Vietnamese   22 | 5 | 15 | $10
Sandwiches 🍽 *Sandwiches*

E Village | 150 E. Second St. (Ave. A) | 212-388-1088
Boerum Hill | 311 Atlantic Ave. (bet. Hoyt & Smith Sts.) | Brooklyn |
718-855-8838 Ⓜ
www.nickyssandwiches.com
"Addictive" *banh mi* sandwiches are the trademark at this "pint-sized"
Vietnamese pair, whose "fresh bread" and "fantastic" fillings are an
"absolute delight" for a "bargain" "quick bite"; their "bare-bones"
storefronts persuade most junkies to "get takeout."

99 Miles to Philly 🍽 *Cheese Steaks*   18 | 7 | 12 | $12
E 50s | 300½ E. 52nd St. (bet. 1st & 2nd Aves.) | 212-308-1308
E Village | 94 Third Ave. (bet. 12th & 13th Sts.) | 212-253-2700 ◗
www.99milestophilly.net
"Damn good" Philly cheese steaks "without the 99-mile drive" turn up
at this "cash-only" East Villager where aficionados order them "with
Cheez Whiz for the real deal"; despite "not much atmosphere" or service, it's popular with "NYU" types given its cheap tabs; N.B. the new
East Midtown satellite opened post-Survey.

Notaro *Italian*   ▽ 18 | 15 | 21 | $38
Murray Hill | 635 Second Ave. (bet. 34th & 35th Sts.) | 212-686-3400 |
www.notaroristorante.com
They "make you feel at home" at this "friendly" Murray Hill "neighborhood" Tuscan in Murray Hill, dishing up "satisfying" "comfort food" in
a "quiet", "cozy" setting abetted by a "fireplace in back"; its "affordable" prices notably include a $20.95 deal for "the early-bird crowd."

Nyonya ◗🍽 *Malaysian*   22 | 12 | 13 | $21
Little Italy | 194 Grand St. (bet. Mott & Mulberry Sts.) | 212-334-3669
(continued)

(continued)

Nyonya

Sunset Park | 5323 Eighth Ave. (54th St.) | Brooklyn | 718-633-0808 |
www.penangusa.com

The "best of Malaysia" is available at this Little Italy–Sunset Park duo
that "covers all the bases" with its "excellent", "properly spiced" offerings; the service is "in a rush" and "they still don't take credit cards",
but it's "hard to argue" with such "dirt-cheap" tabs.

Oceana 🗷 *American/Seafood*   26 | 24 | 24 | $101

E 50s | 55 E. 54th St. (bet. Madison & Park Aves.) | 212-759-5941 |
www.oceanarestaurant.com

It's "all aboard for excellent fish" at this Midtown New American,
which "steers a straight course" with "pristine" seafood, "calm" "luxury
liner" atmospherics and "service above the call of duty"; the $78 prix
fixe–only dinner menu is an "expense-account buster" (so check out the
$28 prix fixe lunch instead), but the "elegance" "will leave you floating."

Ocean Grill *Seafood*   23 | 20 | 21 | $54

W 70s | 384 Columbus Ave. (bet. 78th & 79th Sts.) | 212-579-2300 |
www.brguestrestaurants.com

UWS finatics "would be lost" without Steve Hanson's "vibrant" seafooder, where the "splendid" fish is "fresh enough to swim away" and
there's a "buzz" that swells throughout the "stylish room"; it's "not for
quiet conversation", but the "courteous" staff, "fair" prices and "terrific" brunch are "bound to please", ditto the $25 pre-theater special.

Olives *Mediterranean*   22 | 21 | 20 | $58

Union Sq | W Union Sq. | 201 Park Ave. S. (17th St.) | 212-353-8345 |
www.toddenglish.com

"Todd English doesn't disappoint" at this "upscale" Med in the W Union
Square, where "creative" fare is "well worth" the "expense-account"
pricing (there's also a $24 lunch for bargain-hunters); with a "jumping
social scene" in the bar, "everything is pleasurable" except the "din."

Omai *Vietnamese*   23 | 17 | 19 | $40

Chelsea | 158 Ninth Ave. (bet. 19th & 20th Sts.) | 212-633-0550 |
www.omainyc.com

"Once you've found it" behind an "unmarked exterior", this "compact"
Chelsea Vietnamese aims to please with "terrific" chow served by a

| | FOOD | DECOR | SERVICE | COST |

"helpful" staff; the "spare" setup is "slightly tight", but those apprised of the "modest cost" say "'oh my' is right."

Once Upon a Tart . . . *Coffeehouse* | 20 | 14 | 13 | $16

SoHo | 135 Sullivan St. (bet. Houston & Prince Sts.) | 212-387-8869 | www.onceuponatart.com

Unsurprisingly, the "delicious tarts" "steal the show" at this SoHo cafe, an "old-fashioned" cubbyhole that also vends "inexpensive" sandwiches, salads and other "well-made" bites; given the "close" quarters and scarce service, many opt for outdoor seating or "takeout."

O'Neals' ● *American* | 17 | 16 | 18 | $45

W 60s | 49 W. 64th St. (bet. B'way & CPW) | 212-787-4663 | www.onealsny.com

Lincoln Center attendees "can count on" this "rambling" area "standby" for "ample portions" of "straightforward" Americana at "sensible prices"; the "lively bar" contributes to the "congenial", "pubby" atmosphere, though it's "at its best" once the show-goers "clear out."

Oriental Garden *Chinese/Seafood* | 24 | 12 | 17 | $31

Chinatown | 14 Elizabeth St. (bet. Bayard & Canal Sts.) | 212-619-0085

Seafood "doesn't get any fresher" than when it's plucked "out of the tank" at this "reasonable" Chinatown Cantonese, NYC's No. 1 Chinese, an "old favorite" for "outstanding" eating that includes "high-quality dim sum"; but "abrupt" service and a "simple" space "packed with locals" mean it's "not a place for lingering."

Otto ● *Pizza* | 23 | 19 | 19 | $39

G Village | 1 Fifth Ave. (enter on 8th St., bet. 5th Ave. & University Pl.) | 212-995-9559 | www.ottopizzeria.com

The Batali-Bastianich team's Village enoteca/pizzeria is a "hit" with "the masses", offering fairly priced "designer" pies, "robust" pastas, "unreal gelati" and "incredible" Italian wines in a "raucous" ersatz railway station; it's "jam-packed" with "yuppies", "tourists and the college set", so expect "crazy waits."

Our Place *Chinese* | 20 | 14 | 18 | $34

E 50s | 141 E. 55th St. (bet. Lexington & 3rd Aves.) | 212-753-3900 | www.ourplace-teagarden.com

(continued)

(continued)

Our Place

E 80s | 1444 Third Ave. (82nd St.) | 212-288-4888 | www.ourplaceuptown.com

"Upgrade your Chinese" experience at these separately owned sources of "winning dishes" and "courteous" service, known for "Shanghainese specialties" in Midtown and "weekend dim sum" on the UES; although midpriced, "devout regulars" place them "above the crowd."

Pampano *Mexican/Seafood* 24 | 22 | 21 | $56

E 40s | 209 E. 49th St. (bet. 2nd & 3rd Aves.) | 212-751-4545 | www.modernmexican.com

You'll go far "beyond burritos" at chef Richard Sandoval and tenor Plácido Domingo's "high-end" Midtown Mexican, where the "luscious seafood" menu hits all the right notes (ditto the bargain-priced $26 lunch); "enthusiastic" staffers and a "sunlit upstairs" "make the tab worthwhile"; P.S. the adjacent taqueria sells takeout inspired by the "streets of Mexico."

Pam Real Thai Food ⊅ *Thai* 22 | 9 | 16 | $23

W 40s | 402 W. 47th St. (bet. 9th & 10th Aves.) | 212-315-4441 ●Ⓜ

W 40s | 404 W. 49th St. (bet. 9th & 10th Aves.) | 212-333-7500 www.pamrealthai.com

As advertised, this "Thai-rific" Hell's Kitchen twosome pampers fans of "real-deal" Siamese fare with "splendid" "spicy" cooking that makes it "plenty popular" despite "bare-bones decor" and "amateur" service; it's cash-only, but "so cheap you don't mind."

Papaya King *Hot Dogs* 21 | 4 | 12 | $7

E 80s | 179 E. 86th St. (3rd Ave.) | 212-369-0648 ●⊅

Harlem | 121 W. 125th St. (bet. Lenox & 7th Aves.) | 212-678-4268 Ⓩ⊅

W Village | 200 W. 14th St. (7th Ave. S.) | 212-367-8090 www.papayaking.com

"Bliss in a bun" sums up these "standing-counter" purveyors of grilled "red hots" that "snap" plus "fresh tropical drinks" at prices everyone "can still afford"; you have to "brave" "sleazy" digs and "rub shoulders with who knows who", but you haven't experienced NYC until you try it.

	FOOD	DECOR	SERVICE	COST

Pascalou *French*

20 | 14 | 17 | $43

E 90s | 1308 Madison Ave. (bet. 92nd & 93rd Sts.) | 212-534-7522

"Tiny" but "big-hearted", this Carnegie Hill "shoebox" stays "on the mark" with "wonderful" French bistro recipes and an "upbeat" feel; happily, the "affordable" menu includes a "bargain" "early-bird prix fixe."

Pasha *Turkish*

20 | 18 | 19 | $42

W 70s | 70 W. 71st St. (bet. Columbus Ave. & CPW) | 212-579-8751 | www.pashanewyork.com

This "authentic" Turk "tucked away" on the UWS "entices" with "delightful" cuisine and a "colorful" but "calm" setting that "allows conversation without a megaphone"; with "warm" service, low lights and "fair prices", it's "deservedly popular", especially "for dates."

Pastrami Queen *Deli*

19 | 4 | 12 | $24

E 70s | 1125 Lexington Ave. (bet. 78th & 79th Sts.) | 212-734-1500 | www.pastramiqueen.com

If you "miss the old Jewish delis", this UES "kosher nirvana" supplies "Everest-high" sandwiches stuffed with meats that "melt in your mouth" and "coagulate around your waist"; the decor is "pretty sad" and seating's "limited", so some prefer to "take out."

Patricia's *Italian*

24 | 14 | 20 | $27

Bronx | 1080-1082 Morris Park Ave. (bet. Haight & Lurting Aves.) | 718-409-9069 | www.patriciasmorrispark.com

Bronx | 3764 E. Tremont Ave. (bet. Randall & Roosevelt Aves.) | 718-918-1800 | www.patriciasoftremont.com

When "you don't want to break the bank", the "wholesome" pastas and pizzas at these separately owned Bronx Italians "deliver on taste every time"; considering the "cramped quarters" have almost "no ambiance" besides "sports on the TV", "takeout" is encouraged.

Patroon 🔏 *American/Steak*

20 | 20 | 20 | $66

E 40s | 160 E. 46th St. (bet. Lexington & 3rd Aves.) | 212-883-7373 | www.patroonrestaurant.com

"Join the dark suits" for "business" powwows at Ken Aretsky's weekdays-only Midtowner, a "classy", "conservative" New American enclave for "succulent" steaks, "smooth" service and a "fun bar" scene on the roof; it's "on the pricey side", but you'll "get what you pay for", and there is an inexpensive $27 prix fixe lunch.

| | FOOD | DECOR | SERVICE | COST |

Peanut Butter & Co. *Sandwiches* | 19 | 13 | 15 | $13 |

G Village | 240 Sullivan St. (bet. Bleecker & W. 3rd Sts.) | 212-677-3995 |
www.ilovepeanutbutter.com

"If you're a peanut butter lover", "go gourmet" at this Village empo-
rium that "elevates" PB&J "to an art form" with its "creative" sandwiches; it's "pricey" compared with "your grammar school lunchbox",
but the results are "too yummy to complain."

Peking Duck House *Chinese* | 22 | 15 | 17 | $37 |

Chinatown | 28 Mott St. (bet. Mosco & Pell Sts.) | 212-227-1810
E 50s | 236 E. 53rd St. (bet. 2nd & 3rd Aves.) | 212-759-8260
www.pekingduckhousenyc.com

This "ducky" Chinese duo "can't be beat" for their "succulent", well-
priced house specialty, "skillfully carved right at the table" at both the
"plain-Jane" Midtowner and its "nicer looking" C-Town sire; those who
flock in for the fairly fared fowl feel everything else is "pretty standard."

Penelope ⊄ *American* | 21 | 17 | 19 | $25 |

Murray Hill | 159 Lexington Ave. (30th St.) | 212-481-3800 |
www.penelopenyc.com

"If you seek comfort food", the "winsome staff" at this "cozy" Murray
Hill American serves a "delightful", "well-priced" selection in "cutesy"
"country kitchen" surroundings; it's "popular" with "the girls" despite
"ridiculous brunch lines" and an "annoying" cash-only policy.

Pepe Giallo To Go *Italian* | 21 | 14 | 17 | $26 |

Chelsea | 253 10th Ave. (bet. 24th & 25th Sts.) | 212-242-6055
Pepe Rosso Caffe *Italian*
E 40s | Grand Central | lower level (42nd St. & Vanderbilt Ave.) | 212-867-6054
E Village | 127 Ave. C (8th St.) | 212-529-7747
Pepe Rosso Osteria *Italian*
W 50s | 346 W. 52nd St. (bet. 8th & 9th Aves.) | 212-245-4585
Pepe Rosso To Go *Italian*
SoHo | 149 Sullivan St. (bet. Houston & Prince Sts.) | 212-677-4555
Pepe Verde To Go *Italian*
W Village | 559 Hudson St. (bet. Perry & W. 11th Sts.) |
212-255-2221
www.peperossotogo.com

"Handy" for fill-ups "on the go", these "basic Italians" turn out "down-
to-earth" pastas "in a heartbeat" for an "amazingly" low price; the

	FOOD	DECOR	SERVICE	COST

amenities "leave something to be desired", but for a "tasty", easygoing neighborhood meal these places are a good bet.

Periyali *Greek* | 23 | 20 | 21 | $57 |

Flatiron | 35 W. 20th St. (bet. 5th & 6th Aves.) | 212-463-7890 | www.periyali.com

"Not your run-of-the-mill" taverna, this "civilized" Flatiron "stalwart" "continues to work wonders" with its "deft" "high-end Greek" fare, "quietly stylish" setting and "wonderful service"; Hellenists insist it's "special" enough that the "expensive" outlay is "worth it", while penny-pinchers praise the $26 prix fixe lunch.

Persimmon 🛇 *Korean* | - | - | - | M |

E Village | 277 E. 10th St. (bet. Ave. A & 1st Ave.) | 212-260-9080

Neo-Korean fare takes the spotlight at this tiny new East Villager from a Momofuku alum, whose space consists of a 20-seat communal table ringed by stylish square stools, plus a few more along the open kitchen; it offers a $37 prix fixe-only menu that changes biweekly to focus on a particular ingredient.

Peter's Since 1969 *American*   ▽ | 20 | 16 | 21 | $24 |

Williamsburg | 168 Bedford Ave. (bet. N. 7th & 8th Sts.) | Brooklyn | 718-388-2811 | www.peterssince.com

Irony aside, this recent arrival to Williamsburg delivers on its name with good old-fashioned value, plating up "mouthwatering rotisserie chicken with delicious sides" and other American comfort classics at "affordable" prices; there's no table service, but clean design details like subway-tile walls lend a little savoir faire to an otherwise casual joint.

Pho Bang ⇗ *Vietnamese* | 20 | 6 | 12 | $15 |

Little Italy | 157 Mott St. (bet. Broome & Grand Sts.) | 212-966-3797

Elmhurst | 82-90 Broadway (Elmhurst Ave.) | Queens | 718-205-1500

Flushing | 41-07 Kissena Blvd. (Main St.) | Queens | 718-939-5520

At this Vietnamese noodle threesome they ladle out "big bowls" of "light" but "deeply satisfying" pho soups; "no-decor" settings and "gruff" service are easy to take given the "quick" turnaround and "dirt-cheap" prices.

	FOOD	DECOR	SERVICE	COST

Phoenix Garden ⊄ *Chinese* — 23 | 7 | 12 | $29

E 40s | 242 E. 40th St. (bet. 2nd & 3rd Aves.) | 212-983-6666 |
www.thephoenixgarden.com

It's "nothing to look at", but loyalists "would go any day, anytime" for
the "flavorful", "carefully prepared" Chinese food at this "cheap" BYO
"dive" in the "shadow of Tudor City"; never mind the "depressing" decor and "surly" service – "just sit down and eat."

Pho Viet Huong *Vietnamese* — ∇ 22 | 9 | 13 | $18

Chinatown | 73 Mulberry St. (bet. Bayard & Canal Sts.) |
212-233-8988

In the "no-frills Chinatown" mold, this Vietnamese "standby" delivers
"superior", "bargain"-rate dishes to "tantalize the taste buds"; its noodle
soups are the "highlight" pho sure, but the "extensive menu" boasts
plenty of other choices for a "quick" lunch between court sessions.

Piccolo Angolo Ⓜ *Italian* — 25 | 12 | 20 | $41

W Village | 621 Hudson St. (Jane St.) | 212-229-9177 |
www.piccoloangolo.com

"Genial" owner Renato Migliorini and his "friendly" crew deliver "wonderfully prepared" Italian "red-sauce" staples at this "unpretentious"
Village "favorite"; there's often a "line" and once inside the space is
"tight" and "loud", but for "meatballs the size of your head" and the ut-
most in hospitality, "nothing beats" it.

Ping's Seafood ◗ *Chinese/Seafood* — 21 | 10 | 14 | $26

Chinatown | 22 Mott St. (bet. Bayard & Pell Sts.) | 212-602-9988
Elmhurst | 83-02 Queens Blvd. (Goldsmith St.) | Queens | 718-396-1238

The "tasty Cantonese morsels" and "fresh seafood" at this "chaotic"
Elmhurst-Chinatown duo "outshine" many other "NYC dim sum pal-
aces"; the low-cost cart-borne selection "keeps the adventurous ex-
perimenting", plus the "wait is never long" if you share a table.

Pink Tea Cup ◗⊄ *Soul Food/Southern* — 19 | 11 | 16 | $22

W Village | 42 Grove St. (bet. Bedford & Bleecker Sts.) | 212-807-6755 |
www.thepinkteacup.com

"You ain't a NYer till" you've brunched on "eggs, grits" and the "Elvis
of bacon" at this pink "Village hideaway"; the "affordable" "down-
home Southern" vittles are "satisfying" – "but if you don't like smothered", mosey on ("they'd smother Jell-O if they could").

	FOOD	DECOR	SERVICE	COST

Pio Pio *Peruvian* — 22 | 13 | 16 | $23

E 90s | 1746 First Ave. (bet. 90th & 91st Sts.) | 212-426-5800
Murray Hill | 210 E. 34th St. (bet. 2nd & 3rd Aves.) | 212-481-0034
W 90s | 702 Amsterdam Ave. (94th St.) | 212-665-3000
Bronx | 264 Cypress Ave. (bet. 138th & 139th Sts.) | 718-401-3300
Jackson Heights | 84-13 Northern Blvd. (bet. 84th & 85th Sts.) | Queens | 718-426-1010
Rego Park | 62-30 Woodhaven Blvd. (63rd Ave.) | Queens | 718-458-0606 ⌷
www.piopionyc.com

There's "much to cluck about" at this "boisterous" mini-chain proffering a "Peruvian feast" of "juicy", "sinfully good" rotisserie chicken with "sublime" green sauce and sangria; "who cares" if it's "cramped" – portions are "super-huge" and prices "unbeatable."

Pisticci *Italian* — 24 | 19 | 20 | $34

W 100s | 125 La Salle St. (B'way) | 212-932-3500 | www.pisticcinyc.com
Practically "part of the Columbia curriculum", this "cheery" "subterranean" Italian is "wonderful" for "meeting, talking and just plain enjoying yourself" over "savory", "priced-right" fare; add in "clever" decor and live-jazz Sundays, and it's no wonder the regulars are so "devoted."

Pizza Gruppo *Pizza* — ▽ 24 | 12 | 17 | $19

E Village | 186 Ave. B (bet. 11th & 12th Sts.) | 212-995-2100 |
www.gruppothincrust.com

If "you want thin and crispy, this is it" declare groupies who gobble up the "extra-tasty", "cracker-crusted" pizzas at this "tiny" East Villager; the decor's not much, but it's "cheap and easy", with pleasant service and a "jukebox" as a bonus.

P.J. Clarke's ◐ *Pub Food* — 16 | 15 | 16 | $35

E 50s | 915 Third Ave. (55th St.) | 212-317-1616
P.J. Clarke's at Lincoln Square ◐ *Pub Food*
W 60s | 44 W. 63rd St. (Columbus Ave.) | 212-957-9700
P.J. Clarke's on the Hudson *Pub Food*
Financial District | 4 World Financial Ctr. (Vesey St.) | 212-285-1500
www.pjclarkes.com

"Burgers and beer" "reign supreme" at this midpriced Midtown watering hole that supplies "honest" "bar food" in digs dating from 1884; the "massive" Financial District and Lincoln Center spin-offs are "lively", but their "chainlike" feel "pales in comparison" to the original.

| | FOOD | DECOR | SERVICE | COST |

Public House *Pub Food*   − | − | − | M

E 40s | 140 E. 41st St. (bet. Lexington & 3rd Aves.) | 212-682-3710 |
www.publichousenyc.com

NYC gets its own link of the national franchise with the arrival of this
modestly priced Midtown megapub that's one block south of Grand
Central; since the atmosphere could be Anywhere U.S.A., it's appropriately convenient for commuters.

Pukk *Thai/Vegetarian*   ▽ 23 | 21 | 21 | $21

E Village | 71 First Ave. (bet. 4th & 5th Sts.) | 212-253-2742 |
www.pukknyc.com

Even "full-on carnivores" are "ready to return" for the "cheap", "original and delicious" vegetarian Thai offerings at this East Villager; its
"spacey" decor seems "modeled after" a "YMCA swimming pool", but
"in a good way" – and you "must go see the bathroom."

Pump Energy Food *Health Food*   18 | 5 | 13 | $14

E 50s | Crystal Pavilion | 805 Third Ave. (50th St.) | 212-421-3055 🛇
Flatiron | 31 E. 21st St. (bet. B'way & Park Ave. S.) | 212-253-7676
Garment District | 112 W. 38th St. (bet. B'way & 6th Ave.) | 212-764-2100
W 50s | 40 W. 55th St. (bet. 5th & 6th Aves.) | 212-246-6844
www.thepumpenergyfood.com

"It's no sacrifice" to eat "nutritiously" at these "filling stations" pump-
ing out "tasty", "super-charged" health food and shakes; gym rats less
pumped about "sweating the lines" and walls covered with "pictures
of body builders with biceps bigger than your torso" tend to takeout.

Quantum Leap *Health Food/Vegetarian*   20 | 11 | 17 | $20

E Village | 203 First Ave. (bet. 12th & 13th Sts.) | 212-673-9848
G Village | 226 Thompson St. (bet. Bleecker & W. 3rd Sts.) | 212-677-8050
Flushing | 65-64 Fresh Meadow Ln. (67th Ave.) | Queens | 718-461-1307

"Inspired" "veggie goodness" awaits at this "mellow", "earnest" trio
where regulars "can't get enough" of the "creative" health food; "options are plentiful" (including fish) and "portions satisfying", but before leaping remember that you may "wait an eternity for your order."

Rack & Soul *BBQ/Southern*   19 | 10 | 16 | $26

W 100s | 258 W. 109th St. (B'way) | 212-222-4800 | www.rackandsoul.com
"Honey, these ain't your mamma's biscuits" or BBQ ribs say boosters
of this "dinerlike" Columbia-area Southerner's "super-tasty", "down-

home" grub deemed the "stuff dreams are made of"; still, purists shrug it's best for merely "tiding you over till you can get the real deal."

Rai Rai Ken ●⊖⊖ *Noodle Shop* 21 | 11 | 17 | $15

E Village | 214 E. 10th St. (bet. 1st & 2nd Aves.) | 212-477-7030

For true "Tokyo eating" in the East Village, squeeze into this "friendly", "no-frills" "sliver" of a "noodle counter" and slurp up "delicious", "affordable" "elixirs in ramen form"; the "only things missing" are the "Japanese company men."

Ramen Setagaya ⊖ *Noodle Shop* 20 | 10 | 15 | $18

E Village | 141 First Ave. (bet. 9th St. & St. Marks Pl.) | 212-529-2740

Blows the competition "out of the water" declare devotees of this "austere" link of a Tokyo-based chain that's heating up the East Village "ramen wars" with its "deeply flavored broth" and "chewy noodles"; still, the less-impressed respond "feh" – "too salty."

Rare Bar & Grill *Burgers* 21 | 15 | 17 | $31

G Village | 228 Bleecker St. (bet. Carmine St. & 6th Ave.) | 212-691-7273

Murray Hill | Shelburne Murray Hill Hotel | 303 Lexington Ave. (37th St.) | 212-481-1999

www.rarebarandgrill.com

The "burger sits on the pedestal it deserves" at these "upscale joints" where young carnivores "gorge" on "damn fine" patties and "even better" french fries; other rare refinements include weekend jazz brunches and the Murray Hill branch's "fab rooftop bar."

Rice ⊖ *Eclectic* 19 | 15 | 16 | $22

Gramercy | 115 Lexington Ave. (28th St.) | 212-686-5400

NoHo | 292 Elizabeth St. (bet. Bleecker & Houston Sts.) | 212-226-5775 ●

Dumbo | 81 Washington St. (bet. Front & York Sts.) | Brooklyn | 718-222-9880

Fort Greene | 166 DeKalb Ave. (Cumberland St.) | Brooklyn | 718-858-2700

www.riceny.com

"Multicultural, mix-and-match" rice "every way possible" is the deal at this "unassuming" Eclectic quartet where you choose the components to "create your own dinner"; it's "quick", "cheap" and "good for vegetarians" – and those who cheer "bring on the carbs!"

RUB BBQ *BBQ*

| 20 | 9 | 15 | $28 |

Chelsea | 208 W. 23rd St. (bet. 7th & 8th Aves.) | 212-524-4300 |
www.rubbbq.net

"Real Kansas City BBQ done right", from "righteous ribs" to "lean, savory brisket", keeps this "fairly priced", "no-frills" Chelsea joint jumping; "better show up early", though, because "sometimes they run out
of what you really want."

Saigon Grill ❶ *Vietnamese*

| 21 | 12 | 16 | $25 |

G Village | 91-93 University Pl. (bet. 11th & 12th Sts.) | 212-982-3691
W 90s | 620 Amsterdam Ave. (90th St.) | 212-875-9072

"Heaping plates" of "fresh" Vietnamese eats served "super speedy"
supply a "cheap thrill" at this "popular" pair; they're "crowded and
noisy" and the decor "isn't fetching", yet diners "leave contented."

Saravanaas *Indian*

| ∇ 24 | 10 | 14 | $22 |

Gramercy | 81 Lexington Ave. (26th St.) | 212-679-0204 |
www.saravanaas.com

"Excellent", "real-deal dosas" and other "subtle" South Indian vegetarian vittles are "something to get excited about" at this Gramercy
"diamond in the rough"; patrons happily overlook "poor service",
"crowded tables" and a "plain" space given the "seriously cheap" tabs.

Savann *French/Mediterranean*

| 19 | 15 | 19 | $37 |

W 70s | 414 Amsterdam Ave. (bet. 79th & 80th Sts.) | 212-580-0202 |
www.savann.com

Providing an "oasis" of "quiet" for Upper Westsiders to "sit and talk",
this "homey" French-Med "standby" serves "surprisingly good" eats in
a "comfortably rustic" setting; a staff that "tries hard" and "small
checks" add to the overall "enjoyable" experience.

SEA *Thai*

| 21 | 22 | 17 | $27 |

E Village | 75 Second Ave. (bet. 4th & 5th Sts.) | 212-228-5505 |
www.spicenyc.net
Williamsburg | 114 N. Sixth St. (Berry St.) | Brooklyn | 718-384-8850 |
www.seathairestaurant.com ❶

For "excellent Thai on the cheap", try this "high-energy" duo, whose
"bursting-at-the-seams" East Village location is "not as showy" as
Williamsburg's "nightclub-like" branch; "blasting" music, "hit-or-
miss" service and "crazy-busy" weekends are the deal at both.

	FOOD	DECOR	SERVICE	COST

2nd Ave Deli ◐ *Deli* | 22 | 12 | 16 | $28 |

Murray Hill | 162 E. 33rd St. (bet. Lexington & 3rd Aves.) | 212-689-9000 | www.2ndavedeli.com

Recently transplanted to Murray Hill, this black-and-white-tiled kosher deli remake "captures the spirit of the famous original" with the same "mile-high" pastrami sandwiches ("do I eat it or climb it?") and "gruff" service; the "cramped" interior accounts for the "out-the-door lines" at prime times.

Sette Enoteca e Cucina *Italian* | 19 | 17 | 17 | $38 |

Park Slope | 207 Seventh Ave. (3rd St.) | Brooklyn | 718-499-7767 | www.setteparkslope.com

With "20 wines under $20" and "ever-flowing champagne cocktails" at brunch, the "solid" Southern Italian eats at this Park Sloper taste all the more "satisfying"; even considering "sometimes-shoddy" service and "noisy" environs, it's "perfect for a date", especially in the "pretty" enclosed patio.

Shake Shack *Burgers* | 23 | 13 | 12 | $14 |

Flatiron | Madison Square Park | 23rd St. (Madison Ave.) | 212-889-6600
W 70s | 366 Columbus Ave. (77th St.) | no phone
www.shakeshack.com

"Brilliant" burgers and hot dogs plus "shakes worth every calorie" add up to pure "magic" at this Madison Square Park alfresco "treat", now open year 'round; there's only one "negative" – "half the planet" is "on line", so "check their webcam" or "be prepared" for a "monumental" wait; N.B. the lines may be more bearable at the new UWS satellite.

Sharz Cafe & Wine Bar *Mediterranean* | 19 | 14 | 18 | $40 |

E 80s | 435 E. 86th St. (bet. 1st & York Aves.) | 212-876-7282

"Fine Mediterranean cooking" and a "gazillion affordable wines" are the draw at this "off-the-beaten-path" UES bistro; "yes, it's tiny", and "unhip" too – "nobody's showing off" here, just enjoying the "relaxed" vibe and "terrific value."

Shun Lee Cafe ◐ *Chinese* | 20 | 16 | 18 | $42 |

W 60s | 43 W. 65th St. (bet. Columbus Ave. & CPW) | 212-769-3888 | www.shunleewest.com

"Upscale" dim sum stars at this "busy" Lincoln Center–area Chinese whose "efficient" service makes it perfect for a "before-show bite";

though its "black-and-white checkerboard" digs may be in "need of updating", it's "cheaper" than its "fancier" next-door sibling.

67 Burger *Burgers*
21 | 13 | 16 | $16

Fort Greene | 67 Lafayette Ave. (Fulton St.) | Brooklyn | 718-797-7150 | www.67burger.com

"Mouthwatering, juicy burgers", "hand-cut" fries and an "excellent beer selection" are the hallmarks of this Fort Greene patty palace that's "close to BAM"; the decor may be "industrial" and the mood "frenetic", but no one's complaining given tabs this "cheap."

Smoke Joint *BBQ*
22 | 10 | 16 | $20

Fort Greene | 87 S. Elliot Pl. (Lafayette Ave.) | Brooklyn | 718-797-1011 | www.thesmokejoint.com

'Cue fans "queue up" at this "funky" Fort Greene "cafeteria" for "succulent, tender" BBQ on the "cheap"; its "relaxed", "get-your-own-silverware" vibe includes "juke joint decor" and "harried-but-happy" service, making it "a favorite" "before or after BAM."

Soba-ya *Japanese*
23 | 16 | 19 | $29

E Village | 229 E. Ninth St. (bet. 2nd & 3rd Aves.) | 212-533-6966 | www.sobaya-nyc.com

"Sublime soba" swimming in soups and supported by sybaritic side dishes ensures this "high-quality", "low-key" East Village Japanese is a "favorite"; service can be "rushed", but with its "pleasing" vibe and "inexpensive" tabs, "you can't get near the place during peak hours."

Song ⊅ *Thai*
23 | 17 | 18 | $21

Park Slope | 295 Fifth Ave. (bet. 1st & 2nd Sts.) | Brooklyn | 718-965-1108

"First-class dining at Third World prices" makes this "hip" "sister to Joya" "the joint to hit for delish Thai" in Park Slope; the food's served "efficiently, if not elegantly" in a "minimalist" room that's "crowded" and "raucous", so take "earplugs" or do "takeout."

Sookk *Thai*
∇ 23 | 19 | 17 | $27

W 100s | 2686 Broadway (bet. 102nd & 103rd Sts.) | 212-870-0253

"Unusual" "Thai with a twist of Chinese" (like "eating in Bangkok") makes this "lovely" new sibling to Room Service a "wonderful addition to the UWS"; its "clever", colorful digs are "a bit tight" and the staff "somewhat confused", but given the super-"reasonable" tabs, who cares?

	FOOD	DECOR	SERVICE	COST

Spice Market ◐ *SE Asian* | 22 | 26 | 20 | $59 |

Meatpacking | 403 W. 13th St. (9th Ave.) | 212-675-2322 | www.jean-georges.com

From the "stunning" two-floor setting to the "sublime" Southeast Asian "street vendor" cuisine, Jean-Georges Vongerichten's Meatpacking District "fantasy" market is "a feast for the senses" – and a treat for bargain-hunters, given its $17 bento box lunch special; with "hot" staffers in "racy outfits" serving a "cool" "eye-candy" crowd, it's a "must-visit" – and those downstairs party rooms are a must-stay.

Spicy & Tasty ⊄ *Chinese* | 23 | 8 | 13 | $23 |

Flushing | 39-07 Prince St. (39th Ave.) | Queens | 718-359-1601

The "name says it all" about the "lip-numbingly good", "real-deal" Sichuan cooking at this "Flushing treasure"; the space is "spartan" and service "lax", but to overcome the "language barrier" just "point out what you want" and "dig in."

Spotted Pig ◑ *Gastropub* | 22 | 18 | 16 | $46 |

W Village | 314 W. 11th St. (Greenwich St.) | 212-620-0393 | www.thespottedpig.com

"Pretty people", "celebs" and many of NYC's "top" toques "clamor to get in" to this pleasingly priced Village gastropub for April Bloomfield's "spot-on" Modern European eats; it's "all the rage", so "hurried service" and "killer waits" are a given, unless you "go at off hours" (fortunately, the kitchen's open till 2 AM).

Sripraphai ⊄ *Thai* | 27 | 13 | 16 | $25 |

Woodside | 64-13 39th Ave. (bet. 64th & 65th Sts.) | Queens | 718-899-9599

Once again voted NYC's "champ of Thai food", this "fantabulous" Woodsider offers "outrageously good" dishes with an "incendiary" quotient that's "not for weaklings"; a redo recently "beefed up" its "ho-hum" decor, while the garden remains "wonderful" and the low tabs "incredible", so no surprise, the staff can get "overwhelmed" and there's "often a long wait."

Stand ◑ *Burgers* | 20 | 14 | 16 | $23 |

G Village | 24 E. 12th St. (bet. 5th Ave. & University Pl.) | 212-488-5900

"Delicious" burgers "jazzed up" with "outrageous sides" and "milk-shakes from heaven" (spiked with "spirits") are the draws at this "casual" Village eatery; its "picnic"-style tables are "filled with families and college kids" who, given the "price point", are "not concerned" about service.

Surya *Indian* ▽ | 22 | 16 | 20 | $38

W Village | 302 Bleecker St. (bet. Grove St. & 7th Ave. S.) | 212-807-7770 | www.suryany.com

The "standout" regional Indian eats at this "calm" Village spot taste even better thanks to its classy cocktails and "attentive service"; its "take-out lunch boxes are a deal" at $6.95, but dining in the "peaceful, secluded garden" is the real "plus" given the somewhat plain "mod" interior.

Sushi Yasuda ⊠ *Japanese* | 28 | 21 | 23 | $79

E 40s | 204 E. 43rd St. (bet. 2nd & 3rd Aves.) | 212-972-1001 | www.sushiyasuda.com

"If God were going out for sushi", chef Naomichi Yasuda's "peaceful" Grand Central-area "temple" – once again voted the No. 1 Japanese in NYC – might "be the place" thanks to its "pristine" bites of "pure piscatorial pleasure"; mortals enjoying the "heavenly" experience "relax" in a handsome "minimalist" space attended to by a "polite" staff, while the cost-conscious savor the $23 prix fixe dinner.

Sweet-n-Tart Cafe ●⇹ *Chinese* | 19 | 11 | 13 | $17

Flushing | 136-11 38th Ave. (Main St.) | Queens | 718-661-3380 | www.sweetntart.com

"Fast food, Chinese-style" is the deal at this "cheap", "reliable" Flushing Cantonese "favorite" for "authentic dim sum" and "amazing desserts"; gripes about "seen-better-days" decor have been addressed by a post-Survey overhaul, which also broadened the menu (and may outdate the above ratings).

Tamarind ● *Indian* | 25 | 22 | 22 | $54

Flatiron | 41-43 E. 22nd St. (bet. B'way & Park Ave. S.) | 212-674-7400 | www.tamarinde22.com

Recently renovated, this Flatiron Indian boasts a "calming", "modern" atmosphere and "knowledgeable" service, but it's the "fit-for-a-maharaja" fare that "takes center stage"; yes, "it'll cost you", but then there's always the "wonderful" $24 lunch prix fixe – or the "bargain" next-door tearoom.

	FOOD	DECOR	SERVICE	COST

Tang Pavilion *Chinese* | 22 | 17 | 21 | $39 |

W 50s | 65 W. 55th St. (bet. 5th & 6th Aves.) | 212-956-6888
This "comfortable" Midtown Chinese stalwart's menu of Shanghai delights "changes remarkably little" over time – and that's a "good thing"; its "efficient" staff, "reasonable" prices and location "convenient" to Radio City and City Center make it a no-brainer.

Tao ❶ *Pan-Asian* | 22 | 26 | 19 | $60 |

E 50s | 42 E. 58th St. (bet. Madison & Park Aves.) | 212-888-2288 | www.taorestaurant.com
With its "loud" "dance music", "jaw-dropping" Zen-themed decor (complete with "giant Buddha") and "lively" "young" clientele, this Midtown Pan-Asian "feels more like a club" than a restaurant; the "pricey" food is "surprisingly good", and the $24 prix fixe lunch is quite the bargain.

Tempo *Mediterranean* | 24 | 22 | 23 | $49 |

Park Slope | 256 Fifth Ave. (bet. Carroll St. & Garfield Pl.) | Brooklyn | 718-636-2020 | www.tempobrooklyn.com
What with the "divine" Med cuisine, "extraordinary" wines, "thoughtful" service and "date-place" ambiance, it's a "mystery" that this "classy" prix fixe–only Park Sloper "isn't packed every night" – especially since its multicourse options are offered at "Brooklyn prices"; P.S. it's possible to order à la carte in the "beautiful" bar area.

Teresa's *Diner* | 19 | 11 | 14 | $22 |

Brooklyn Heights | 80 Montague St. (Hicks St.) | Brooklyn | 718-797-3996
"Big portions" of traditional diner fare and "hearty" Polish "comfort" dishes, perfect for a "casual brunch", have the locals returning often to this Brooklyn Heights stalwart; though a meal "won't set you back financially", "slow", "gruff" service and "tired" digs may set you back emotionally.

Thai Pavilion *Thai* | ▽ 21 | 12 | 20 | $23 |

Astoria | 37-10 30th Ave. (37th St.) | Queens | 718-777-5546 | www.thaipavilionny.com
"Not your usual" neighborhood Thai, this Astoria veteran's "delicious", "spicy" dishes are delivered "with care and pride" at "really local prices"; its "not-very-large" digs boast "no bells and whistles", so takeout or delivery are always worth considering.

	FOOD	DECOR	SERVICE	COST

Tía Pol *Spanish* 　　24 | 15 | 19 | $40
Chelsea | 205 10th Ave. (bet. 22nd & 23rd Sts.) | 212-675-8805 |
www.tiapol.com
A "tiny place that's big on food", this "lively" Chelsea *tapería* offers
an "excellent array of Spanish nibbles" paired with "top-notch"
wines; "long waits" are the norm, but "if you can squeeze in", try
"everything" – though bear in mind that those "little snacks" "can add
up" if you're not careful.

Tierras Colombianas ⑦ *Colombian* 　20 | 11 | 17 | $25
Astoria | 33-01 Broadway (33rd St.) | Queens | 718-956-3012
Jackson Heights | 82-18 Roosevelt Ave. (82nd St.) | Queens | 718-426-8868
"When you want something stick-to-your-ribs", these "friendly"
Queens "bargains" fill the bill with "flavorful", "down-to-earth"
Colombian dishes big enough "to feed a small horse"; the "dinerlike"
digs are "nothing fancy", but you'll "eat like a king" – or three.

Tom's ⊠⑦ *Diner* 　　20 | 17 | 26 | $16
Prospect Heights | 782 Washington Ave. (Sterling Pl.) | Brooklyn |
718-636-9738
"Service is a matter of pride" at this "classic" 1930s Prospect Heights
coffee shop famed for its "friendly" vibe and "killer brunches"; its "old-
school" offerings like egg creams and lime rickeys match the "throwback" decor – as do the pleasingly low tabs.

Tribeca Grill *American* 　　22 | 20 | 21 | $60
TriBeCa | 375 Greenwich St. (Franklin St.) | 212-941-3900 |
www.tribecagrill.com
Back in 1990, Drew Nieporent and Robert De Niro put TriBeCa "on the
map" tablewise with this "casual", "high-quality" New American;
years later, it "still shines" for "excellent people-watching" and a hard-
to-beat $29 set-price lunch.

Turkish Cuisine ◐ *Turkish* 　　19 | 13 | 18 | $32
W 40s | 631 Ninth Ave. (bet. 44th & 45th Sts.) | 212-397-9650 |
www.turkishcuisinenyc.com
Its "multitude" of "tasty", budget-oriented dishes make this "friendly"
Hell's Kitchen Turk a "reliable" choice pre- or post-curtain; for more
elbow room and less "rushed" service, "go when everyone else is
at the theater."

	FOOD	DECOR	SERVICE	COST

Utsav *Indian* | 21 | 19 | 19 | $38 |

W 40s | 1185 Sixth Ave., 2nd fl. (bet. 46th & 47th Sts.) | 212-575-2525 | www.utsavny.com

"Hidden" in Midtown, this "upmarket" Indian is a welcome "change of pace" for "pre-theater" dining thanks to its "relaxing" second-floor setting and staffers providing guidance with the "novice-friendly" fare; the lunch buffet is a "sampler's delight" at $17.95.

Veselka *Ukrainian* | 18 | 11 | 14 | $20 |

E Village | 144 Second Ave. (9th St.) | 212-228-9682 ◐
E Village | First Park | 75 E. First St. (1st Ave.) | 347-907-3317 🍴
www.veselka.com

"Portions are large" and prices "low" at this "bustling" "throwback to the old Ukrainian East Village"; it plies its "comforting" fare 24/7 and is equally "beloved" for "hangover brunches" and "pierogi at 2 AM", "spotty" service and "dinerlike" digs notwithstanding; P.S. the "Little Veselka" kiosk on East First Street serves a smaller sampling of "noshes."

ViceVersa 🅱 *Italian* | 22 | 21 | 22 | $53 |

W 50s | 325 W. 51st St. (bet. 8th & 9th Aves.) | 212-399-9291 | www.viceversarestaurant.com

Perhaps the "most pleasant of the Theater District" standbys, this "reliable" Italian "continues to shine" with "thoughtfully prepared" dishes, "polished" service and a "sleek, sophisticated" room; bonus points go to the "romantic back garden" and its $35 prix fixe dinner.

VietCafé 🅱 *Vietnamese* | ▽ 22 | 17 | 17 | $33 |

TriBeCa | 345 Greenwich St. (bet. Harrison & Jay Sts.) | 212-431-5888 | www.viet-cafe.com

Vietnamese specialties "modern" and "traditional" are a "cut above" at this "relaxed", "trendy"-looking TriBeCa eatery offering solid "value" and some popular "lunchtime options" (including "the best" "Viet sandwiches"); fans just wonder why this place "isn't busier" at dinner given the reasonable tabs.

Village *American/French* | 19 | 18 | 19 | $44 |

G Village | 62 W. Ninth St. (bet. 5th & 6th Aves.) | 212-505-3355 | www.villagerestaurant.com

Half "French bistro", half "local tavern", this Villager is a "warm", "dependable" "standby" for "pleasant" Franco-American fare and "reasonably priced wines"; "regulars" stop for a drink at the "cheerful" bar then head back to a "table under the wonderful skylight."

Virgil's Real Barbecue ◑ *BBQ*

20 | 13 | 16 | $34

W 40s | 152 W. 44th St. (bet. B'way & 6th Ave.) | 212-921-9494 | www.virgilsbbq.com

"Yes, you can find" "succulent BBQ" near Times Square at this "barnlike" joint brimming with "tourists and locals" "pigging out" on "affordable" eats and using "towels as napkins"; all in all, it's a "fun, fast, messy" time, even if service blows "hot and cold."

Vivolo ⊠ *Italian*

19 | 17 | 20 | $49

E 70s | 140 E. 74th St. (bet. Lexington & Park Aves.) | 212-737-3533 | www.vivolonyc.com

This "charming townhouse" Italian is an "old-school" "favorite" among "mature" UESers who appreciate its "calm" vibe and "terrific $29 early-bird" deal; critics, who cry "time warp", say it "could be more inventive", but "regulars" retort "it's been around a long time for good reason."

Vong *French/Thai*

22 | 23 | 21 | $64

E 50s | 200 E. 54th St. (3rd Ave.) | 212-486-9592 | www.jean-georges.com

"Still delightfully different", Jean-Georges Vongerichten's Midtown French-Thai offers "perfectly balanced" fusion dishes in "beautiful, almost otherworldly" surroundings staffed by an "attentive" team; yes, tabs can get "hefty", but the $20 lunch prix fixe is a serious "value."

Waldy's Wood Fired Pizza *Pizza*

22 | 10 | 15 | $17

Chelsea | 800 Sixth Ave. (bet. 27th & 28th Sts.) | 212-213-5042 | www.waldyspizza.com

"Gourmet pizza" with "crisp wood-fired crusts" and "fresh, interesting" toppings but "without the attitude" is the deal at Waldy Malouf's "tiny" Chelsea pie place; limited seating and service sometimes "like a *Seinfeld* episode" are part of the package.

Walker's ◑ *Pub Food*

17 | 13 | 17 | $29

TriBeCa | 16 N. Moore St. (Varick St.) | 212-941-0142

"Comfy as your favorite jeans", this TriBeCa "institution" is "beloved" for its "reliable" "burger-and-beer" eats at "honest" prices; it's a "wonderful holdover" from the area's pre-"yuppie" days, with a "neighborhood-tavern" vibe that affords "lots of local color."

	FOOD	DECOR	SERVICE	COST

West Branch ⓂAmerican | - | - | - | M |

W 70s | On the Ave. Hotel | 2178 Broadway (77th St.) | 212-777-6764 |
www.thewestbranchnyc.com

UWS favorite son Tom Valenti (Ouest) brings conviviality to the West
Side via this casual new brasserie featuring a cover-all-bases New
American menu served in wood-lined, burgundy-hued digs; in a nod to
the current financial times, the pricing is gratifyingly gentle.

'wichcraft *Sandwiches* | 20 | 11 | 14 | $16 |

Chelsea | Terminal Warehouse | 269 11th Ave. (bet. 27th & 28th Sts.) |
212-780-0577
E 40s | 245 Park Ave. (47th St.) | 212-780-0577 🖧
E 40s | 555 Fifth Ave. (46th St.) | 212-780-0577 🖧
Flatiron | 11 E. 20th St. (bet. B'way & 5th Ave.) | 212-780-0577
G Village | 60 E. Eighth St. (Mercer St.) | 212-780-0577
Murray Hill | Equinox | 1 Park Ave. (33rd St.) | 212-780-0577
SoHo | Equinox | 106 Crosby St. (Prince St.) | 212-780-0577
TriBeCa | 397 Greenwich St. (Beach St.) | 212-780-0577
W 40s | Bryant Park | Sixth Ave. (bet. 40th & 42nd Sts.) | 212-780-0577
W 50s | 1 Rockefeller Plaza (on 50th St., bet. 5th & 6th Aves.) | 212-780-0577
www.wichcraftnyc.com

"Sublime sandwiches" with "exceptional ingredients" and "sophisticated
combinations" are the "magic" of this burgeoning mini-chain from
Craft's Tom Colicchio; service can be "slow" and the "price-portion ratio"
can "seem unfair", but for "upscale brown-bagging" it "can't be beat."

Wildwood Barbeque *BBQ* | 17 | 17 | 17 | $39 |

Flatiron | 225 Park Ave. S. (bet. 18th & 19th Sts.) | 212-533-2500 |
www.brguestrestaurants.com

Steve Hanson's B.R. Guest (Dos Caminos, Ruby Foo's, etc.) "does the
BBQ thang" at this new "rustic-chic" "barn" of a Flatironer that's packing
in a "young" crowd; opinions are split on its smokehouse fare ("luscious"
vs. "disappointing"), but all agree the "busy bar scene" is a hoot.

Wo Hop ◑⇍ *Chinese* | 21 | 5 | 13 | $18 |

Chinatown | 17 Mott St. (Canal St.) | 212-267-2536

A Chinatown "greasy spoon, er chopstick" that "never changes", this
circa-1938, all-night "standby" keeps churning out "terrific", "dirt-
cheap" Cantonese dishes via "disinterested waiters" in a "harshly lit"
basement that resembles a "Communist-bloc bus station."

| | FOOD | DECOR | SERVICE | COST |

Wondee Siam *Thai* | 23 | 8 | 16 | $22 |
W 40s | 641 10th Ave. (bet. 45th & 46th Sts.) | 212-245-4601
W 50s | 792 Ninth Ave. (bet. 52nd & 53rd Sts.) | 212-459-9057 ∉
W 50s | 813 Ninth Ave. (bet. 53rd & 54th Sts.) | 917-286-1726
"Delectable", "dirt-cheap" Thai that's "as close to the real thing as you can get" earns this Hell's Kitchen trio a loyal fan base; aficionados happily ignore the "nonexistent decor" and variable service and focus instead on the "wondee-ful" eats.

X.O. ∉ *Chinese* | 19 | 10 | 13 | $17 |
Chinatown | 96 Walker St. (bet. Centre & Lafayette Sts.) | 212-343-8339
Little Italy | 148 Hester St. (bet. Bowery & Elizabeth St.) | 212-965-8645
At this "Hong Kong–style" dim sum duo, the "vast" menu is so "affordable", you can "sample" lots "without breaking the budget"; it's a "cheap", "fun" time, as long as you don't mind the "divey" digs.

Yuva *Indian* | ▽ 22 | 17 | 19 | $46 |
E 50s | 230 E. 58th St. (bet. 2nd & 3rd Aves.) | 212-339-0090 | www.yuvanyc.com
"Sublimely spiced" specialties satisfy subcontinental sympathizers at this "upscale" East Midtown Indian, where the "charming" (if sometimes "slow") staff delivers "authentic" standards in vaguely "corporate" quarters; sealing the deal are relatively "reasonable" prices and a "fantastic" $14 lunch buffet.

Zabar's Cafe *Deli* | 19 | 6 | 11 | $17 |
W 80s | 2245 Broadway (80th St.) | 212-787-2000 | www.zabars.com
Acolytes "schlep" to the UWS for bagels, nova and other "affordable" "taste-of-NY" delights at this legendary deli; sure, it's notorious for its "grouchy" service and "crowded" space, but for the vast majority of surveyors, it's simply "fulfilling."

Zarela *Mexican* | 21 | 16 | 18 | $43 |
E 50s | 953 Second Ave. (bet. 50th & 51st Sts.) | 212-644-6740 | www.zarela.com
Usually "packed", this Eastsider showcases Zarela Martinez's "artful" Mexican specialties (including a $17 set-price lunch) inside a "lively" bi-level space complete with a "bustling" street-level bar; insiders warn "watch it" when it comes to those "wicked" margaritas, or "you won't be able to climb upstairs" to eat.